Dairy Diary Favourites

100 MUCH-LOVED RECIPES FROM THE PAST 35 YEARS

DAIRY COOKBOOK

Contents

4   Introduction

Weekday Eating

8   Soups & Snacks

10   Children's Tea

26   Easy Healthy Meals

With Friends & Family

52   Relaxed Lunch

100   Evening Entertaining

136   Great Bakes

170   Decadent Drinks

172   Index

Introduction

The Dairy Diary is one of the most recognised and best-loved British books in the UK today. Its first edition, in 1982, was an enormous success and subsequent editions went on to sell millions of copies – over 30 million during the last 35 years – which is something of a publishing phenomenon.

First Launched by the Milk Marketing Board, it was originally, and for many years, sold exclusively by milkmen. It's still supplied by thousands of milkmen and women but as fewer households now have milk delivered it's also sold online.

The Dairy Diary continues with the same values as the very first edition and is packed full of useful home information, as well as fascinating features and, of course, its famous practical and delicious triple-tested recipes.

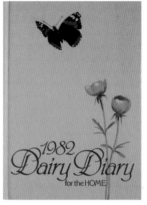

The Dairy Diary has sold over 30 million copies.

There are many consumers who have collected the Dairy Diary since it first began and now have 35 editions crammed into their bookshelves.

Others have used it for years but lost precious books during house moves and other life events. As a result, many readers request long-lost recipes on a regular basis. In response to these requests we have created this compendium of favourite Dairy Diary recipes, for everyone to enjoy.

Favourite recipes

The Dairy Diary has showcased over two thousand recipes and it would be impossible to include all of them in one book. This cookbook features 100 of the best and most-requested recipes, including at least one from every edition. The terms 'best' and 'favourite' are subjective and will vary with personal taste but we hope you will find your favourite recipes and perhaps discover some more.

In every case we have tried to keep the essence of the original recipe, but as ingredients and tastes have changed over 35 years, those changes have necessitated some small tweaks to ensure that each and every recipe uses readily available ingredients, works perfectly and, of course, tastes delicious.

The chapters

The book has been split into two sections; the first features speedy weekday meals for children and also for adults and the second has a wealth of recipes perfect for entertaining – either for relaxed lunches, impressive suppers or simply a delicious piece of cake to serve with coffee.

Triple-tested

All the recipes in this book have been tested at least three times, so they are guaranteed to work each and every time and taste superb. We hope you enjoy trying them.

Recipe Notes

Nutritional information
Nutritional information has been calculated per portion or item. Where there are portion variations, e.g. serves 6-8, the analysis given is based on the larger number.

Measurements
Both metric and imperial measurements are given. Follow either set of measures but not a mix of both.

Eggs
Large eggs and medium-sized vegetables are recommended unless otherwise stated.

Nuts
Recipes using nuts or nut products are not suitable for young children or for those with a nut allergy.

At-risk groups
Certain at-risk groups, such as babies, pregnant women, sick or elderly people should avoid eating raw or lightly cooked eggs.

Makes 12 slices
Time 3 hours plus cooling
Per slice: 475 Kcal
xxg fat (xg saturated)

Simnel C

F **V**

Butter 175g (6oz)
Caster sugar 175g (6oz)
Eggs 3, beaten
Plain flour 250g (9oz), sifted
Mixed spice 1 tsp
Mixed dried fruit 450g (1lb)
Milk 2 tbsp
Apricot jam 3 tbsp
Marzipan 250g (9oz), rolled out to an 18cm (7in) diameter circle, 1cm (½in) thick, plus extra to make 11 marzipan balls
Sugar-coated chocolate eggs to decorate (optional)

Preheat the oven to an 18cm (7in) round baking paper.

Cream the butter and fluffy. Gradually beat i spice and mix to a sm dried fruits and milk a

Spoon the mixture ir for 1 hour, then reduce 150°C/130°fan/Gas 2 a or until the cake is firm

Leave to cool in the ti onto a wire rack to coo

Brush the top of the c the marzipan circle on t fluted effect.

V Suitable for vegetarians, provided an appropriate cheese or yogurt is used.

F Suitable for freezing.

The QR code under the ingredients list can be scanned with your smartphone to provide you with a handy shopping list.

The list is embedded in the QR code so no internet access is required.

Weekday Eating

Soups & Snacks

8   Chicken & Corn Soup

8   Broccoli & Apple Soup

8   Spanish Tomato Soup

8   Cheese & Tomato Tasty

9   Toastie Yogurt Surprise

9   Savoury Croissants

9   Eggy Bread BLT

9   Pepperami Muffins

Children's Tea

10   Homemade Fish Fingers

12   Chicken Kievs

14   Pasta Supper

16   Pigs in Blankets

18   Cottage Pie with Baked Beans

20   Stripy Jelly

22   Candy Rice Pudding

24   Cinnamon Pancakes with Blueberry Sauce

Easy Healthy Meals

26   Cauliflower & Potato Curry

28   Peanut Noodles

30   Perfect Potatoes

32   Chilli Beans with Wedges

34   Curried Supper Eggs

36   Sea Bass with Asparagus & Roasted Potatoes

38   Gourmet Beans on Toast

40   Eight-Minute Prawns

42   Lemon Chicken

44   Lamb Keema Curry

46   Liver Special

48   Chilli Beef Tacos

Chicken & Corn Soup

Serves 4   Time 15 minutes
Per portion: 263 Kcal, 8.6g fat (4.1g saturated)

Butter 15g (½oz)
Spring onions 1 bunch, trimmed and sliced
Creamed sweetcorn 400g can
Frozen sweetcorn 110g (4oz)
Cooked chicken 175g (6oz), shredded
Chicken stock 300ml (½ pint)
Milk 450ml (¾ pint)
Light soy sauce 1 tbsp
Egg 1, beaten
Coriander leaves to garnish (optional)

Melt the butter in a large saucepan and fry the spring onions for 30 seconds. Add the sweetcorn, chicken and stock. Bring to the boil, cover and simmer for 5 minutes.

Stir in the milk and soy sauce and bring almost to the boil. Add the beaten egg while stirring gently, to form egg threads. Cook until the egg has set, but do not boil.

Garnish with coriander leaves, if you like and serve immediately.

Broccoli & Apple Soup

Serves 4   Time 40 minutes
Per portion: 260 Kcal, 24g fat (14g saturated)

Broccoli 1 large head, approx. 300g (11oz)
Butter 50g (2oz)
Red onion 1, peeled and chopped
Dessert apples 2, peeled, cored and chopped
Vegetable stock 750ml (1¼ pints)
Salt and freshly ground black pepper
Double cream 90ml (3fl oz)

Discard the tough stem from the broccoli and coarsely chop the rest.

Melt the butter in a large saucepan, add the onion and apples, cover and cook for 10 minutes. Add the stock and broccoli, bring to the boil, cover and simmer for 15 minutes.

Leave to cool slightly, then transfer to a food processor or blender and purée until smooth. Season to taste. Return to the saucepan and reheat gently. Stir in the cream and serve hot.

Spanish Tomato Soup

Serves 4   Time 60 minutes
Per portion: 185 Kcal, 9.8g fat (6g saturated)

Butter 25g (1oz)
Onions 225g (8oz), peeled and sliced
Ripe tomatoes 900g (2lb), chopped (including skin and seeds)
Paprika ½ tsp
Dry sherry 90ml (3fl oz)
Sugar 1 tbsp
Salt 1 tsp
Chopped mint 4 tbsp or **dried mint** 1½ tsp
Single cream 6 tbsp
Mint leaves to garnish (optional)

Melt the butter in a large saucepan and gently fry the onions until softened but not browned.

Add the tomatoes, paprika, sherry, sugar, salt and mint, stir well, cover and simmer for 45 minutes, stirring occasionally.

Leave to cool slightly, then transfer to a food processor or blender and purée until smooth. Strain through a sieve into a saucepan and add enough water to give the desired consistency. Reheat gently and serve hot, garnished with cream and mint leaves.

Cheese & Tomato Tasty

Serves 4   Time 15 minutes
Per portion: 400 Kcal, 28g fat (16g saturated)

Butter 25g (1oz)
Tomatoes 4, skinned and finely chopped
Spring onions 6, trimmed and chopped
Cheddar cheese 175g (6oz), grated
Double Gloucester cheese 50g (2oz), grated
Eggs 2, beaten
Hot toast or baked potatoes to serve

Melt the butter in a small saucepan, add the tomatoes and spring onions and cook, stirring, for 5 minutes until most of the liquid has evaporated.

Mix together the cheeses and the eggs. Add to the tomatoes and stir continuously over a low heat until the mixture thickens.

Serve hot as a topping for toast or baked potatoes. Or serve cold as a sandwich filling.

Toastie Yogurt Surprise

Serves 4   Time 10 minutes
Per portion: 459 Kcal, 25g fat (14g saturated)

Wholemeal bread 8 slices
Butter 40g (1½oz)
Mango chutney 4 tbsp
Low-fat natural yogurt 250g (9oz)
Eggs 2, beaten
Lancashire cheese 150g (5oz), crumbled
Freshly ground black pepper

Preheat the grill. Toast the bread lightly on both sides. Spread with butter, going right up to the edges, then spread with chutney.

Mix together the yogurt, eggs and cheese. Season with pepper. Spread the yogurt mixture over the toast and place under a moderate grill until golden and just bubbling. Serve hot.

Savoury Croissants

Serves 4   Time 20 minutes
Per portion: 436 Kcal,
26g fat (14g saturated)

Butter 25g (1oz)
Onion ½, peeled and finely chopped
Mushrooms 110g (4oz), sliced
Cooked ham 110g (4oz), chopped
Plain flour 2 tsp
Soured cream 75ml (2½fl oz)
French mustard 2 tsp
Salt and freshly ground black pepper
Croissants 4
Cheddar cheese 50g (2oz), grated

Preheat the oven to 200°C/180°fan/Gas 6.

Melt the butter in a saucepan and fry the onion and mushrooms for 3 minutes, stirring frequently. Stir in the ham and flour and cook for 1 minute.

Remove the pan from the heat and stir in the soured cream and mustard. Season to taste.

Split the croissants in half and place the bottom halves onto a baking tray. Spoon on the filling and sprinkle with cheese. Top with croissant halves and bake for 7 minutes. Serve hot.

Eggy Bread BLT

Serves 1   Time 15 minutes
Per portion: 577 Kcal, 39g fat (7.5g saturated)

Vegetable oil 2 tbsp
Smoked back bacon 2 slices
Tomato 1, cut in half
Egg 1
Milk 2 tbsp
Salt and freshly ground black pepper
Salad leaves small handful
White bread 2 thick slices

Heat 1 tablespoon of the oil in a frying pan and fry the bacon and tomato until the bacon is done to your liking and the tomato is softened. Remove from the pan and keep warm.

In a shallow bowl, beat together the egg and milk with a little seasoning.

Put the bacon, tomato halves and salad leaves on one slice of bread and cover with the other slice to make a sandwich. Press together firmly. Place the sandwich in the egg mixture and turn over so it gets completely coated.

Heat the remaining oil in the frying pan and fry the sandwich for 2–3 minutes on each side until golden. Serve immediately.

Pepperami Muffins

Serves 2   Time 15 minutes
Per portion: 419 Kcal, 19g fat (10g saturated)

Muffins 2
Tomato chutney 4 tbsp
Mushrooms 40g (1½oz), sliced
Red Leicester cheese 40g (1½oz), grated
Wensleydale cheese 40g (1½oz), grated
Stick of snack salami 25g (1oz), sliced
Chopped parsley to garnish (optional)

Preheat the grill. Split the muffins and toast the outside of each.

Spread the chutney over the untoasted sides. Arrange the mushrooms on top of the chutney. Mix together the cheeses and salami and divide between the muffins.

Grill until the cheese is bubbling. Serve hot, sprinkled with parsley, if using.

Shun tasteless shop-bought fish finger
and treat your little ones to this delicou
homemade version from the 2002 Diary

Homemade Fish Fingers

Makes 8

Time 15 minutes

Per fish finger: 144 Kcal
6g fat (0.6g saturated)

Cut the fish into eight strips and season with salt and pepper.

Sprinkle the flour in a shallow dish, put the beaten egg in another dish and the breadcrumbs in another. Dust each fish finger in the flour, dip into the egg and then toss in the breadcrumbs, making sure they are completely coated.

Heat the vegetable oil in a deep-fat fryer or deep wide saucepan.

Carefully lower the fish fingers into the hot oil. You may need to do this in batches. Cook for 2–3 minutes until the crumb coating is crisp and golden. Drain on kitchen paper and serve with beans, broccoli and a squirt of ketchup, if you like.

Thick cod or haddock fillet 250g (9oz), skinned

Salt and freshly ground black pepper

Plain flour 2 tbsp

Egg 1, beaten

Dry white breadcrumbs 110g (4oz)

Vegetable oil for deep-fat frying

Broccoli, baked beans and ketchup to serve (optional)

Cook's TIPS To check that the oil is hot enough, use a cook's thermometer – it should read 180-190°C/350-375°F. Or, drop a square of bread into the oil; if the oil bubbles around it immediately the oil is hot enough.

Scan the **QR Code** with a smartphone for an ingredients shopping list

Makes 2

Time 35–40 minutes

Per portion: 428 Kcal

19g fat (9.7g saturated)

Chicken Kievs

Skinless chicken breasts
2 small

Butter 25g (1oz)

Garlic 1 clove, peeled and crushed

Chopped parsley 1 tbsp

Plain flour 1 tbsp

Grated Parmesan cheese 1 tbsp

Egg 1, beaten

Cornflakes 50g (2oz), crushed

Cherry tomatoes and peas to serve (optional)

Preheat the oven to 180°C/160°fan/Gas 4.

Cut a small slit horizontally in each chicken breast. Mix together the butter, garlic and parsley. Push this mixture into the chicken pockets. Secure with cocktail sticks.

In a shallow dish mix together the flour and Parmesan. Put the beaten egg in another dish and the cornflakes in another. Dust the chicken in the flour, then dip into the egg and finally the cornflakes.

Place on a baking tray and bake for 20–25 minutes until cooked through (no pink juices appear when pierced with a knife) and golden. Remove the cocktail sticks and serve with cherry tomatoes and peas, or other vegetables of your choice.

Scan the **QR Code** with a smartphone for an ingredients shopping list

Cook's TIPS

The cornflakes can be crushed by putting them into a plastic bag and rolling with a rolling pin. Or get the children involved and get them to crush the cornflakes with clean hands on a baking tray.

A real retro classic – these gorgeous crunchy chicken Kievs from the 2002 Dairy Diary will delight adults and children alike.

How can something so simple be so delicious? This pasta dish from the 1990 Diary is a real family favourite.

Pasta Supper

Serves 2 adults and 3 children

Time 20 minutes

Per portion: 529 Kcal
31g fat (17g saturated)

Cook the tagliatelle according to the packet's instructions.

Melt the butter in a saucepan, add the oil and cook the onion for about 4 minutes until soft.

Add the ham and frozen peas and cook for a further 4 minutes.

Add the drained tagliatelle, cream and half of the cheese. Toss together and serve immediately sprinkled with the remaining cheese.

Dried tagliatelle 250g pack

Butter 40g (1½oz)

Olive oil 1 tbsp

Onion 1 small, peeled and finely chopped

Ham 110g (4oz), cut into strips

Frozen peas 110g (4oz)

Single cream 150ml (¼ pint)

Cheddar cheese 110g (4oz), grated

Cook's TIPS

Dried tagliatelle has been used here but it can be tricky for little ones to twiddle around a fork. For young diners you might like to use pasta twists or shells instead that can be scooped up with a spoon.

Scan the **QR Code** with a smartphone for an ingredients shopping list

Makes 6
Time 40-50 minutes
Per portion: 328 Kcal
22g fat (9.7g saturated)

Pigs in Blankets

Medium-sliced white bread
6 slices

Butter 50g (2oz)

Tomato ketchup 4 tsp

Mild Dijon mustard 1 tsp

Cumberland sausages 6, skins removed

Preheat the oven to 200°C/180°fan/Gas 6. Cut the crusts off each slice of bread, then gently roll out each slice, using a rolling pin, to make it thinner.

In a small saucepan, gently heat the butter and tomato ketchup together until melted, then stir in the mustard.

Brush some of the butter mixture over one side of each slice of bread, then place a sausage diagonally across each one. Bring the opposite corners up and over the sausages to meet in the centre, and secure with wooden cocktail sticks.

Place on a baking tray, brush with the remaining butter mixture and bake for 30–40 minutes until the sausages are cooked. Check halfway through cooking and if the bread is browning too much cover with strips of foil.

Scan the **QR Code** with a smartphone for an ingredients shopping list

Cook's TIPS

The points of the bread tend to brown more quickly in the oven than the rest of the bread, so check on the progress once or twice during cooking and cover with strips of foil if needed to stop them browning too much.

Perfect for outdoor feasts and teatime treats, these crisp wrapped sausages from the 2007 Diary are a popular choice with everyone.

This popular twist on a British classic is taken from the 2008 Dairy Diary and is a hearty dish that's really simple to prepare.

Cottage Pie with Baked Beans

Serves 2 adults and 3 children
Time 1 hour 20 minutes
Per portion: 659 Kcal
31g fat (13g saturated)

Heat the olive oil in a large frying pan, add the onion and carrots and cook for about 5 minutes until softened.

Add the beef to the pan and continue cooking until the meat is lightly browned. Stir in the stock and herbs and bring to the boil. Turn down the heat and simmer for 20 minutes.

Meanwhile, boil the potatoes in water for 15-20 minutes until cooked.

Preheat the oven to 190°C/170°fan/Gas 5.

Drain the potatoes and mash with butter.

Spoon half the beef mixture into a 1.25 litre (2 pint) baking dish, then add the baked beans and the remaining beef. Cover with mashed potatoes, smooth and mark into swirls with a fork. Brush with egg, if using. Place on a baking tray and cook for 45 minutes or until browned. Serve immediately with peas, if you like.

Olive oil 1 tbsp

Onion 1 large, peeled and finely chopped

Carrots 2 large, peeled and cut into small dice

Lean minced beef 500g (1lb 2oz)

Beef stock 150ml (¼ pint)

Mixed dried herbs 1 tbsp

Potatoes 900g (2lb), peeled and quartered

Butter 25g (1oz)

Baked beans 415g can

Egg 1 small, beaten with 1 tbsp water to glaze (optional)

Peas to serve (optional)

You could make this earlier in the day and reheat when required. Or spoon into individual foil containers, cool, wrap in clingfilm, label and freeze ahead. Defrost in the fridge overnight and reheat a portion for 30 minutes.

Scan the **QR Code** with a smartphone for an ingredients shopping list

Serves 6 children
Time 15 minutes plus chilling
Per portion: 139 Kcal
3.1g fat (1.9g saturated)

Stripy Jelly

Custard powder 2 tbsp

Milk 300ml (½ pint)

Strawberry jelly 135g packet

Whipped cream and jelly beans to decorate

Blend the custard powder with a little cold milk. Bring the remaining milk to the boil and pour onto the mixture, stirring well. Return to the pan and bring back to the boil, stirring. Remove from the heat and leave to cool.

Make up the jelly according to the packet's instructions. Pour a third of the jelly into a jug, stir in the custard and mix well.

Pour half the remaining jelly into a 900ml (1½ pint) glass dish and place the dish in a bowl filled with ice. Chill until set. Pour half the custard mixture on top and chill in ice as before until set. Repeat the layers with the remaining mixture, chilling until set. If the remaining jelly is starting to set, warm in the microwave for 10-20 seconds to soften.

Just before serving, decorate with whipped cream and jelly beans.

Scan the **QR Code** with a smartphone for an ingredients shopping list

Cook's TIPS

If you are in a hurry, pour the first layer of jelly into the dish and freeze for 15 minutes to set quickly. Just make sure that you use a heavy duty glass dish. For decoration buy jelly beans with only natural colours and flavours.

Perfect for a midweek birthday treat, this pretty jelly from 1990 will be a popular choice with all little children.

This caramel-flavoured rice pudding from the 2012 Dairy Diary is easy to prepare and will quickly become a firm family favourite.

Candy Rice Pudding

Serves 2 adults and 3 children

Time 35 minutes

Per portion: 179 Kcal

6g fat (2.8g saturated)

Put the milk, rice and sugar in a pan. Bring to the boil, stirring. Cover and simmer for 30 minutes until the rice is cooked, stirring occasionally.

Break up the candy bar and stir into the rice. Serve hot or cold.

Milk 600ml (1 pint)
Pudding rice 50g (2oz)
Caster sugar 2 tsp
Caramac candy bar 50g (2oz)

Vary the chocolate bar; add your child's favourite – diced Crunchy bar, Milky Bar or Mars Bar could also be used.

Scan the **QR Code** with a smartphone for an ingredients shopping list

Serves 6 children or 3 adults

Time 20 minutes

Per portion: 323 Kcal
7.9g fat (2.2g saturated)

Frozen blueberries 350g packet

Cornflour 1 tsp

Caster sugar 25g (1oz)

Fresh orange juice 2 tbsp

Plain flour 110g (4oz)

Ground cinnamon ¼ tsp

Egg 1

Milk 300ml (½ pint)

Sunflower oil 1 tbsp

Vanilla ice cream to serve

Cinnamon Pancakes with Blueberry Sauce

Tip the blueberries into a pan and add the cornflour, caster sugar and orange juice. Heat gently, stirring occasionally, until the juices have thickened and there is no taste of cornflour.

Meanwhile, sift the flour and cinnamon into a bowl. Make a well in the centre and add the egg. Whisk into the flour and then gradually whisk in the milk.

Wipe a small non-stick frying pan with oil and heat. Add a ladleful of batter, swirl around the pan, and cook until just set. Carefully turn over (or toss if you're brave) and cook the other side. Continue with the remaining batter to make 6 pancakes.

Serve the pancakes with the blueberry sauce and vanilla ice cream.

Scan the **QR Code** with a smartphone for an ingredients shopping list

Cook's TIPS

Any soft fruit can we used in this recipe; choose your favourite. If using red berries you could serve with a berry ice cream.

Pancakes are a perennial favourite and they taste particularly delicious in this dish from the 2014 Dairy Diary, served with blueberries and ice cream.

Packed full of flavour but quick enough to cook mid-week, this 2014 recipe is a great way of getting three of your five-a-day.

Cauliflower & Potato Curry

Serves 4
Time 40 minutes
Per portion: 224 Kcal
7g fat (0.8g saturated)

Heat the oil in a large saucepan and sauté the onion for 4 minutes until softened. Add the garlic and cook for a further minute.

Add the potatoes and stock, bring to the boil, then cover and simmer for 10 minutes.

Add the beans, cauliflower and baby corn and cook for a further 10 minutes.

Stir in the curry paste and cook for 2 minutes.

Serve with pilau rice and warmed naan bread, if you like.

Olive oil 1 tbsp

Onion 1, peeled and sliced

Garlic 1 clove, peeled and crushed

Potatoes 500g (1lb 2oz), peeled and cut into chunks

Vegetable stock 1.25 litres (2 pints)

Fine green beans 110g (4oz), trimmed and sliced

Cauliflower ½, broken into florets

Baby corn 175g (6oz), halved

Curry paste 2-3 tbsp

Pilau rice and naan bread to serve (optional)

Cook's TIPS There is a wide range of curry pastes in the supermarket so buy the strength that you prefer – from mild korma to hotter balti curry pastes.

Scan the **QR Code** with a smartphone for an ingredients shopping list

Serves 2

Time 15 minutes

Per portion: 474 Kcal
17g fat (3.1g saturated)

Peanut Noodles

Sesame oil 1 tbsp

Courgette 1, cut into thin sticks

Carrots 2, peeled and cut into thin sticks

Baby corn 125g (4½oz), halved

Mushrooms 110g (4oz), sliced

Straight-to-wok noodles 300g pack

Milk 4 tbsp

Sweet chilli sauce 1 tbsp

Crunchy peanut butter 2 tbsp

Coriander sprigs to garnish (optional)

Heat the oil in a wok and stir-fry the vegetables for about 5 minutes.

Add the noodles and warm through for 2 minutes.

Meanwhile, put the milk, sweet chilli sauce and peanut butter in a bowl and microwave on full power for 30–40 seconds or alternatively heat gently in a small pan. Whisk together.

Just before serving, stir the peanut sauce into the noodles and vegetables. Spoon into warmed bowls and serve garnished with coriander, if using.

Scan the **QR Code** with a smartphone for an ingredients shopping list

Cook's
TIPS

If you are feeling very hungry then you could also stir-fry some prawns or thinly sliced chicken breast before adding the vegetables.

*Who needs a take-away when homemade can taste
this good? Super-speedy, healthy and simply delicious,
this 2012 Dairy Diary recipe ticks all the right boxes.*

Baked potatoes needn't be boring. These parcels of delight from 1989 mix sweetcorn, egg and herbs with cheese for a scrumptious combination.

Perfect Potatoes

Serves 4

Time 1 hour

Per portion: 342 Kcal
17g fat (9.6g saturated)

Cook the potatoes in the microwave for 5-10 minutes while the oven heats up then bake in the oven at 200°C/180°fan/Gas 6 for 30-45 minutes until crisp on the outside and soft on the inside.

Stand for 5 minutes. Preheat the grill.

Cut a thin slice horizontally from the top of each potato and scoop most of the potato into a bowl. Mix with the soft cheese, boiled eggs, sweetcorn, chives and half the Cheddar then spoon back into the potato shells.

Place the potatoes in a shallow ovenproof dish and sprinkle with the remaining cheese. Place under the hot grill until golden brown. Serve hot with salad and cherry tomatoes, if you like.

Baking potatoes 4, scrubbed and pricked with a fork

Soft cheese 150g (5oz)

Eggs 2, hard-boiled, shelled and chopped

Canned sweetcorn 75g (3oz)

Snipped chives 2 tbsp

Cheddar cheese 50g (2oz), grated

Mixed salad and cherry tomatoes to serve (optional)

Cook's TIPS

While plain soft cheese tastes good you might also like to try a flavoured one, perhaps garlic and herb or crushed peppercorn.

Scan the **QR Code** with a smartphone for an ingredients shopping list

Serves 4

Time 45 minutes

Per portion: 438 Kcal
16g fat (7g saturated)

Chilli Beans with Wedges

Baking potatoes 4, scrubbed
and cut into wedges

Cayenne pepper 1 tsp

Olive oil 2 tbsp

Cheddar cheese 110g (4oz),
grated

Onion 1, peeled and chopped

Red pepper 1, deseeded and
chopped

Mixed beans in spicy sauce
400g can, drained

Red kidney beans 400g can,
drained

Chopped tomatoes with herbs
400g can

Tomato purée 1 tbsp

Tabasco sauce to taste
(optional)

**Salt and freshly ground black
pepper**

Preheat the oven to 200°C/180°fan/Gas 6.

Toss the potato wedges with the cayenne pepper
and 1 tablespoon of the oil in a large roasting tin.
Bake for 25–30 minutes until golden. In the last 5
minutes, sprinkle with the grated cheese.

Meanwhile, heat the remaining oil in a large
saucepan and fry the onion for 5 minutes. Add the
red pepper and fry for a further 2–3 minutes. Stir in
the beans, tomatoes and purée. Bring to the boil and
simmer for 7–8 minutes until thickened. Add a little
Tabasco, if using, and seasoning to taste.

Serve the beans with the cheesy wedges.

Scan the
QR Code with a
smartphone for
an ingredients
shopping list

Cook's
TIPS

If you happen to have a couple of cooked sausages left
in the fridge, then slice them thinly and stir into the chilli
beans when adding the chopped tomatoes.

*Make as mild or spicy as you like – this hearty
dish from the 2003 Dairy Diary is sure to
warm up the coldest of evenings.*

This unusual combination of ingredients from the 1986 Diary just works! For a quick meat-free meal this recipe is perfect.

Curried Supper Eggs

Serves 2
Time 25 minutes
Per portion: 437 Kcal
22g fat (10g saturated)

Melt the butter in a saucepan and sauté the onion and the curry powder until the onion has softened.

Stir in the flour and cook for 2 minutes. Gradually add the milk, stirring all the time. Add the chutney and sultanas. Cover and simmer for 5 minutes.

Cut the eggs in half and add to the sauce. Serve hot on a bed of rice, garnished with coriander and with naan bread, if you like.

Butter 25g (1oz)

Onion 1 small, peeled and sliced

Curry powder 2 tsp

Plain flour 1 tbsp

Milk 225ml (8fl oz)

Mango chutney 3 tbsp

Sultanas 25g (1oz)

Eggs 4, hard-boiled and shelled

Basmati rice, naan bread and chopped coriander to serve (optional)

Scan the **QR Code** with a smartphone for an ingredients shopping list

Cook's TIPS

For nut fans, add a little oil to the saucepan before you make the sauce and gently fry a spoonful of flaked almonds until golden. Remove to a plate before you fry the onions. Sprinkle on the almonds just before serving.

Serves 2

Time 45 minutes

Per portion: 372 Kcal
20g fat (2.8g saturated)

Sea Bass with Asparagus & Roasted Potatoes

Mini new potatoes 250g (9oz), scrubbed

Olive oil 3 tbsp

Lemon 1, grated zest and juice

Asparagus 250g bundle, trimmed

Salt and freshly ground black pepper

Sea bass fillets 2

Chopped flat-leaf parsley 2 tbsp

Preheat the oven to 200°C/180°fan/Gas 6.

Put the potatoes in a pan of salted water, bring to the boil, then simmer for 5 minutes. Drain and tip into a roasting tin with 2 tablespoons of the oil and the lemon zest. Roast for 20 minutes. Add the asparagus, stir and return to the oven for 10 minutes or until the vegetables are tender.

Meanwhile, heat the remaining oil in a non-stick frying pan. Season the fish and score the skin three times with a knife. Fry the fish skin side down for 4 minutes or until the skin is crisp, then turn and cook for 1 more minute or until cooked through.

Sprinkle the lemon juice and parsley over the fish and serve with the potatoes and asparagus.

Scan the **QR Code** with a smartphone for an ingredients shopping list

Cook's
TIPS

Sea bass is readily available in all large supermarkets, but the humble mackerel can also be cooked in the same way and can bought ready filleted – or get the fishmonger to do it for you.

A decadent but totally hassle-free recipe from 2015 for a delicious weekday dinner.

Not just for lunch – this must-try version of beans on toast, with tuna and cheese, from the 2008 Dairy Diary will fill you up until tomorrow.

Gourmet Beans on Toast

Serves 2
Time 20 minutes
Per portion: 576 Kcal
23g fat (8g saturated)

Preheat the grill. Gently heat the baked beans in a small pan on the hob.

Mix the tuna with the mayonnaise and chives.

Toast the bread on one side, then turn over and very lightly toast the other side. Spread the tuna mixture evenly over each slice of toast (right up to the edges).

Spoon the baked beans over the tuna, sprinkle with cheese and cook under the grill until the cheese is melted and lightly browned. Add the tomato slices and cook for just 1 minute. Serve hot garnished with a few chives.

Baked beans 400g can

Tuna in spring water 160g can, drained and flaked

Mayonnaise 2 tbsp

Snipped chives 1 tbsp, plus extra to garnish

Rustic bread 2 large thick slices

Cheddar cheese 50g (2oz), grated

Tomato 4–6 slices

Scan the **QR Code** with a smartphone for an ingredients shopping list

Cook's TIPS

Transfer a supermarket pot of chives into a larger pot and keep on the windowsill. With regular watering it will continue to grow and give you a handy supply of chives to snip and sprinkle when needed.

Eight-Minute Prawns

Butter 25g (1oz)

Spring onions 6, trimmed and chopped

Garlic 3 cloves, peeled and crushed

Dried herbes de Provence 2 tsp

Dry sherry 5 tbsp

Lemon juice 1 tbsp

Worcestershire sauce 2 tsp

Cooked tiger prawns 400g (14oz)

Double cream 125ml (4fl oz)

Basmati rice and lemon wedges to serve (optional)

Paprika to dust

Melt the butter in a frying pan, then add the spring onions, garlic and herbs. Fry for 3 minutes.

Add the sherry, lemon juice and Worcestershire sauce, stir well and then add the prawns. Cook for 2 minutes and then add the cream. Reduce the heat and cook for 2 minutes.

Serve hot, with rice and lemon wedges, if you like, and a little paprika dusted over the dish.

Scan the **QR Code** with a smartphone for an ingredients shopping list

Cook's TIPS

Use ordinary prawns if you cannot find tiger prawns and if you don't have any dry sherry then add a splash of dry white wine instead. You could use dried or fresh chopped parsley rather than mixed herbs.

This 1997 recipe blends sherry, herbs and Worcestershire sauce with cream to provide a rich but quick-and-easy sauce for the succulent prawns.

From the 2013 Dairy Diary – this baked lemon chicken topped with crisp pancetta and served with golden potato wedges makes an absolutely gorgeous meal.

Lemon Chicken

Serves 4

Time 1¼ hours

Per portion: 426 Kcal
20g fat (6.9g saturated)

Preheat the oven to 190°C/170°fan/Gas 5 and put a baking tray in to heat.

Boil the potato wedges for 5 minutes. Drain well and add to the baking tray with 2 tablespoons of the oil. Squeeze the lemon wedges over the potatoes and add to the tray along with the garlic and thyme. Roast near the bottom of the oven for 50 minutes, turning occasionally, until crisp and brown.

Meanwhile, put the chicken in a roasting tin and season with salt, pepper and nutmeg. Place a piece of ham on each chicken breast and put two lemon slices on top. Drizzle with the remaining oil and bake in the oven above the potatoes for 20 minutes. Pour in the stock and bake for a further 20 minutes.

Transfer the chicken and potatoes to warmed plates. Whisk the crème fraîche into the pan juices and pour over the chicken. Serve with broccoli and sugar snap peas, if you like.

Potatoes 4 medium, peeled and cut into wedges

Olive oil 3 tbsp

Lemons 2, 1 cut into 6 wedges and the other cut into 8 slices

Garlic 4 cloves (not peeled)

Thyme sprigs a few

Chicken breasts (skin on) 4

Salt and freshly ground black pepper

Freshly grated nutmeg a pinch

Parma ham 4 slices

Chicken stock 150ml (¼ pint)

Crème fraîche 4 tbsp

Broccoli and sugar snap peas to serve (optional)

Cook's TIPS Choose equal-sized chicken breasts to ensure they will all be cooked at the same time. To check, insert a skewer into the thickest part of one of the breasts – the juices should run clear with no hint of pink when cooked.

Scan the **QR Code** with a smartphone for an ingredients shopping list

Serves 4

Time 1 hour

Per portion: 335 Kcal
18g fat (7.8g saturated)

Lamb Keema Curry

Onion 1, peeled and chopped

Garlic 2 cloves, peeled and chopped

Root ginger 2.5cm (1in), peeled and grated

Minced lamb 500g (1lb 2oz)

Chopped tomatoes 400g can

Cumin 2 tsp

Turmeric 1 tsp

Garam masala 1 tbsp

Chilli powder ½-1 tsp

Raisins 50g (2oz)

Frozen peas 50g (2oz)

Basmati rice, naan bread, fat-free Greek yogurt and fresh mint to serve (optional)

Gently fry the onion, garlic and ginger with the minced lamb until softened and the meat is browned all over.

Pour in the tomatoes with 100ml (3½fl oz) water and all the spices. Cover and simmer gently for 30 minutes.

Add the raisins and frozen peas and cook for a further 15 minutes.

Serve on a bed of rice topped with yogurt and shredded mint, and with naan bread, if you like.

Scan the **QR Code** with a smartphone for an ingredients shopping list

Minced beef, even minced turkey, could be mixed with the spice blend above for a tasty weekday supper.

Rich but mildly spiced, this scrumptious storecupboard curry from the 2016 Diary uses everyday ingredients – just add mince.

Melt-in-the-mouth lamb's liver cooked with vegetables and apple, from 1990, provides you with an easy meal packed with iron.

Liver Special

Serves 4
Time 20 minutes
Per portion: 374 Kcal
20g fat (9.6g saturated)

Mix the flour and curry powder in a large plastic bag, add the liver and shake to coat in the flour. Melt the butter in a large frying pan, add the liver and fry for 3 minutes.

Add the onion and pepper and cook for 3 minutes. Gradually add the milk and cook, stirring, until the sauce thickens, boils and is smooth.

Stir in the sweetcorn and sliced apple and heat through. Serve hot, with rice and sprinkled with parsley, if using.

Plain flour 50g (2oz)

Curry powder ½ tsp

Lamb's liver 450g (1lb), cut into strips

Butter 50g (2oz)

Onion 1, peeled and sliced

Green pepper 1, deseeded and diced

Milk 400ml (14fl oz)

Sweetcorn 198g can, drained

Dessert apple 1, peeled, cored and sliced

Long grain rice to serve (optional)

Chopped parsley to garnish (optional)

Scan the **QR Code** with a smartphone for an ingredients shopping list

Cook's
TIPS

This recipe has just a hint of curry flavour, so for those who like their food spicy, up the amount of curry powder to suit your palate or serve with a spoonful of hot chutney on the side.

Serves 4

Time 40 minutes

Per portion: 467 Kcal
22g fat (5g saturated)

Chilli Beef Tacos

Olive oil 1 tbsp

Onion 1, peeled and finely chopped

Garlic 1–2 cloves, peeled and crushed

Extra-lean minced beef 450g (1lb)

Hot chilli powder ½–1 tsp

Chopped tomatoes 400g can

Red kidney beans 400g can, drained and rinsed

Salt and freshly ground black pepper

Taco shells 12, warmed as directed on packet

Crisp lettuce, finely shredded, to serve

Soured cream 2–3 tbsp, to serve

Cheddar cheese, grated, to serve

Preheat the oven to 180°C/160°fan/Gas 4. Heat the olive oil in a large lidded frying pan, add the onion and cook gently for 5 minutes until softened.

Increase the heat, add the garlic and beef and cook, stirring, until the beef is browned all over.

Stir in the chilli powder, tomatoes and beans. Bring to the boil, stirring, then reduce the heat, cover and cook gently for 20 minutes. Season to taste.

Serve the taco shells filled with lettuce, the chilli beef and bean mixture and topped with soured cream and grated cheese.

Scan the **QR Code** with a smartphone for an ingredients shopping list

Cook's TIPS

You might like to serve the chilli beef and all the trimmings in a warmed soft flour tortilla. Or spoon over baked ordinary or sweet potatoes.

*Make mince more exciting with these tasty
Chilli Beef Tacos from the 2008 Dairy Diary –
the whole family will love them.*

With Friends & Family

Relaxed Lunch

52 Vegetarian Moussaka

54 Family Fish Pie

56 Baked Salmon

58 Spicy Tuna Plait

60 Roast Chicken with Cheese & Peanut Stuffing

62 Chicken & Broccoli Lasagne

64 Chicken & Asparagus Pie

66 Turkey en Croûte

68 Roast Pork with Fanned Potatoes & Treacle-Glazed Red Cabbage

70 Pork Crumble

72 Sausage & Leek Supper

74 Sausagemeat Yorkshire

76 Lamb Crown Roast

78 Minced Lamb Pie

80 Boeuf Stroganoff

82 Frozen Christmas Pudding

84 Chocolate Maple Yule Log

86 Chocolate Pear Flan

88 Banana Cream Pie

90 Pear & Ginger Trifle

92 Hot Swiss Trifle

94 Rustic Raspberry Crumble

96 Butterscotch Apple Pie

98 Calypso Puddings

Evening Entertaining

100 Bacon Wraps

102 Mushroom Ramekins

104 Smoked Salmon & Dill Filo Tarts

106 Chicken Liver Pâté

108 Ham & Cheese Soufflé

110 Hollandaise Salmon

112 Pesto Chicken with Roasted Potatoes

114 Stuffed Pork Fillet

116 Kofta Curry with Naan Bread

118 Steak en Croûte

120 Two Cheese Fondue and Chocolate Fondue

122 Iced Mocha Soufflé

124 Raspberry Amaretto Trifle

126 White Chocolate Cheesecake

128 Strawberry Puffs

130 Easy Fruit Brulée

132 Queen of Puddings

134 Double Lemon Puddings

Great Bakes

136	Irish Soda Bread
138	Savoury Muffins
140	Dainty Iced Gingerbread
142	Crunchy Peanut Brittle
144	Cappuccino Cakes
146	Auntie Lou's Bread Pudding
148	Christmas Flapjacks
150	Mince Pies with Marzipan
152	Mincemeat Bakewell Squares
154	Banana & Pecan Cake
156	Summer Fête Lemon Cake
158	Orange Cake
160	Boiled Fruit Cake
162	Streusel Cake
164	Spiced Apple Cake
166	Coffee Battenberg
168	Simnel Cake

Decadent Drinks

170	Minty Lemon Sorbet Tea
170	Fruity Gin
170	Tropical Fruit Shake
170	Piña Colada
170	Peach Cream Liqueur
171	Perfect Peach
171	Hot Pear Milk
171	Hazelnut Hot Chocolate
171	Spiced Hot Chocolate
171	After Eight Milk

Serves 4

Time 1¼ hours

Per portion: 626 Kcal
51g fat (17g saturated)

Vegetarian Moussaka

Olive oil approx. 125ml (4fl oz)

Onions 350g (12oz), peeled and sliced

Aubergines 2, cut into 5mm (¼in) slices lengthways

Courgettes 2, cut into 5mm (¼in) slices lengthways

Feta cheese 75g (3oz), crumbled

Mozzarella cheese 150g (5oz), sliced

Mixed dried herbs 1 tbsp

Salt and freshly ground black pepper

Plum tomatoes 225g (8oz), sliced

Butter 25g (1oz)

Plain flour 25g (1oz)

Milk 300ml (½ pint)

Egg 1, white only

Parmesan cheese 50g (2oz), grated

Mixed salad to serve (optional)

Preheat the oven to 190°C/170°fan/Gas 5. Preheat the grill.

Heat 3 tbsp of the olive oil in a frying pan, add the onions and cook for 5 minutes or until softened.

Brush the aubergine and courgette slices on both sides with olive oil and cook, in batches if necessary, under a hot grill until softened and lightly browned.

Lay the aubergines, onions and courgettes in a 2 litre (3½ pint) ovenproof dish. Sprinkle the feta and mozzarella, herbs, salt and pepper over the vegetables and top with the tomato slices.

Melt the butter in a saucepan, stir in the flour and milk and bring to the boil, stirring continuously. Remove from the heat. Whisk the egg white until stiff, fold into the sauce and pour over the tomatoes. Sprinkle with Parmesan and bake for 30–40 minutes until golden brown. Serve immediately with a mixed salad, if liked.

Scan the
QR Code with a smartphone for an ingredients shopping list

Cook's
TIPS

When buying cheese, check that it has the vegetarian symbol as those made with a rennet starter will not be suitable for vegetarians.

Perfect for meat-free days, this delicious Med-inspired moussaka from 2007 is packed full of colourful vegetables.

A real family favourite, this comforting 1992 fish pie is topped with creamy potato and swede mash and nutty Red Leicester.

Family Fish Pie

Serves 4

Time 55 minutes

Per portion: 502 Kcal
21g fat (11g saturated)

Boil the potatoes and swede in water for 10-15 minutes until cooked.

Meanwhile, cook the eggs until hardboiled, cool then shell and chop.

Preheat the grill. Put the butter, flour and milk into a saucepan and heat, stirring continuously, until the sauce thickens, boils and is smooth. Add the fish, peas and sweetcorn and cook for 2–5 minutes until the fish is just cooked. Stir in the eggs and parsley and transfer the mixture to an ovenproof dish and keep warm.

Mash the potatoes and swede with a little milk until smooth. Season to taste, then spoon over the fish mixture. Sprinkle with the cheese and place under a hot grill for a few minutes until the cheese has melted. Serve hot.

Potatoes 350g (12oz), peeled and diced

Swede 225g (8oz), peeled and diced

Eggs 2

Butter 50g (2oz)

Plain flour 50g (2oz)

Milk 600ml (1 pint), plus extra for mashing

Smoked haddock 450g (1lb), skinned and cubed

Frozen peas 110g (4oz)

Sweetcorn 198g can, drained

Chopped parsley 1 tbsp

Salt and freshly ground black pepper

Red Leicester cheese 50g (2oz), grated

Cook's TIPS

Most supermarkets now sell fish pie mix which has smoked haddock, salmon and white fish and this could be used in place of the smoked haddock.

Scan the **QR Code** with a smartphone for an ingredients shopping list

Baked Salmon

Serves 4

Time 40 minutes

Per portion: 465 Kcal
35g fat (11g saturated)

Salmon fillets 4, each approx. 150g (5oz), skin removed

Lemon ½, juice only

Fresh dill 15g (½oz)

Butter 20g (¾oz)

Salt and freshly ground black pepper

Cucumber ½, thinly sliced

White wine vinegar 2 tbsp

Caster sugar 1 tsp

Chives 15g (½oz), finely snipped

Chopped watercress 2 tbsp, plus sprigs to garnish

Soft cheese 110g (4oz)

Light mayonnaise 2 tbsp

Steamed new potatoes to serve (optional)

Preheat the oven to 180°C/160°fan/Gas 4. Line a large baking tray with foil.

Place the salmon fillets on the foil, drizzle with the lemon juice, sprinkle with a little torn dill, dot with the butter and season with salt and pepper.

Enclose the salmon in the foil then bake in the oven for 25-30 minutes or until the fish flakes easily and is even in colour when pressed with a knife.

Meanwhile, add the cucumber slices to a bowl with the vinegar, sugar and a little salt and pepper. Reserve a few more dill sprigs for garnish, chop the rest and add half to the cucumber and the remainder to a second bowl. Add half the chives to the cucumber and the rest to the second bowl. Gently toss the cucumber together and set aside.

Add the chopped watercress, soft cheese and mayonnaise to the bowl of herbs and stir together until well mixed. Spoon into a serving bowl.

Stir the cucumber once more then spoon onto a large shallow platter. Arrange the cooked salmon on top then garnish with the watercress sprigs. Serve with the sauce and new potatoes, if using.

Scan the **QR Code** with a smartphone for an ingredients shopping list

Cook's TIPS

Thick cut pieces of smoked cod loin could also be cooked in the same way in the foil then served with the sauce on a bed of stir-fried or microwaved spinach.

Perfect for a buffet lunch, these salmon fillets with cucumber and a creamy sauce from the 2007 Dairy Diary are a welcome change from the ubiquitous cheese sandwiches.

With coronation-like flavour, this midly spiced tuna parcel from 1990 makes a wonderful lunch for family or friends.

Spicy Tuna Plait

Serves 4

Time 55 minutes

Per portion: 762 Kcal
55g fat (29g saturated)

Preheat the oven to 200°C/180°fan/Gas 6. Lightly grease a 900g (2lb) loaf tin.

Mix together the crème fraîche, curry powder, cornflour, seasoning, tuna, sultanas, walnuts (if using), apple and parsley.

Roll out the pastry to 30 x 35cm (12 x 14in) and make diagonal cuts in the pastry one third in from the edge on each side, about 2.5cm (1in) apart.

Carefully lift the pastry into the prepared tin and spoon in the tuna filling. Brush the edges lightly with egg, then fold in the narrow edges at each end. Then fold in the strips, alternating right and left until the filling is covered. Brush with the remaining egg.

Bake for 30–35 minutes until the pastry is golden brown and crisp.

Loosen the edges with a knife and then remove from the tin. Leave to cool on a wire rack. Serve cold with vegetable sticks and tomatoes, if you like, or as part of a buffet.

Crème fraîche 250ml tub

Mild curry powder 2 tsp

Cornflour 2 tsp

Salt and freshly ground black pepper

Tuna in brine 340g can, drained and flaked

Sultanas 25g (1oz)

Walnuts 25g (1oz), chopped (optional)

Dessert apple 1, peeled, cored and diced

Chopped parsley 2 tbsp

Puff pastry 350g (12oz)

Egg 1, beaten

Crunchy vegetable sticks and cherry tomatoes to serve (optional)

Cook's
TIPS

If you are a bit short of time then just wrap the pastry around the filling like a parcel and slash the top several times with a small sharp knife.

Scan the **QR Code** with a smartphone for an ingredients shopping list

Serves 4–6

Time 1¾–2¼ hours

Per portion: 621 Kcal
44g fat (15g saturated)

Roast Chicken with Cheese & Peanut Stuffing

Fresh breadcrumbs 75g (3oz)

Cheddar cheese 110g (4oz), grated

Celery 1 stick, chopped

Salted peanuts 50g (2oz), chopped

Onion 1 small, peeled and chopped

Salt and freshly ground black pepper

Egg 1, beaten

Lemon juice 2 tsp

Whole chicken approx. 1.6kg (3½lb)

Butter 25g (1oz)

Unsmoked streaky bacon 6 rashers

Paprika to sprinkle

Dried parsley to sprinkle

Roast potatoes and vegetables to serve (optional)

Preheat the oven to 200°C/180°fan/Gas 6.

Mix the breadcrumbs, cheese, celery, peanuts and onion in a bowl. Season lightly with pepper and bind with egg and lemon juice, then use to stuff the chicken. Make stuffing balls with any excess mixture and set aside.

Place the chicken in a roasting tin, dot with the butter, season with salt and pepper and cover the breast with the bacon. Cover loosely with foil and bake for 1½–2 hours, depending on the stuffed weight of the bird. See the cook's tip below. For the last 30 minutes of cooking time, remove the foil and take the bacon off the chicken, baste with the pan juices and sprinkle the breast with paprika and parsley. Add the stuffing balls to the roasting tin and return to the oven.

Leave to rest in a warm place for 10 minutes before carving. Serve with roast potatoes and vegetables, if you like.

Scan the **QR Code** with a smartphone for an ingredients shopping list

Cook's TIPS

Weigh the stuffed chicken and cook for 20 minutes per 450g (1lb) plus 30 minutes. You could also cook roast potatoes in the tin with the chicken.

Liven up Sunday lunch with this delicious and decadent 1982 Diary roast chicken served with peanut stuffing.

This much-loved recipe from the 1994 Dairy Diary combines creamy chicken with broccoli and sweetcorn for the lasagne filling.

Chicken & Broccoli Lasagne

Serves 4
Time 1½ hours
Per portion: 662 Kcal
23g fat (12g saturated)

Steam the chicken breasts over a pan of boiling water for about 20 minutes or until the juices run clear when the thickest part is pierced with a knife. Remove from the pan and dice.

Preheat the oven to 190°C/170°fan/Gas 5. Lightly grease a 25 x 20cm (10 x 8in) ovenproof dish.

Melt the butter in a pan and fry the onion for 5 minutes. Stir in the flour and cook for 2 minutes. Gradually stir in the milk and the stock cube. Heat, stirring continuously, until the sauce thickens, boils and is smooth. Cook for 2–3 minutes.

Remove from the heat and stir in the chicken, broccoli, sweetcorn, herbs and seasoning.

Soak the lasagne sheets in a shallow bowl of boiling water for 2 minutes or until softened.

Spread a thin layer of the sauce in the base of the greased dish. Cover with two sheets of lasagne. Repeat the layers of sauce and lasagne once more, and finish with a layer of sauce. Sprinkle with cheese and bake for 35 minutes. Serve immediately with salad, if you like.

Chicken breasts 4

Butter 50g (2oz)

Onion 1, peeled and sliced

Plain flour 50g (2oz)

Milk 900ml (1½ pints)

Chicken stock cube 1, crumbled

Small broccoli florets 225g (8oz), blanched in boiling water for 2–3 minutes, then rinsed in cold water and drained

Sweetcorn 110g (4oz)

Mixed dried herbs 1 tsp

Salt and freshly ground black pepper

Fresh lasagne 4 sheets

Red Leicester cheese 50g (2oz), grated

Mixed salad to serve (optional)

Cook's TIPS At Christmas, use up some of the small pieces of cooked leftover turkey in this lasagne instead of the chicken.

Scan the **QR Code** with a smartphone for an ingredients shopping list

Serves 4–6

Time 55 minutes

Per portion: 523 Kcal
28g fat (14g saturated)

Chicken & Asparagus Pie

Butter 25g (1oz)

Carrots 2, peeled and diced

Baby onions or shallots 8, peeled

Button mushrooms 110g (4oz)

Plain flour 25g (1oz)

Wholegrain mustard 1 tsp

Chicken stock cube 1, crumbled

Milk 450ml (¾ pint)

Cooked chicken 450g (1lb), cut into strips

Asparagus tips 100g pack

Salt and freshly ground black pepper

Single cream 4 tbsp

Puff pastry 225g (8oz)

Egg 1, beaten

Preheat the oven to 200°C/180°fan/Gas 6.

Melt the butter in a saucepan and sauté the carrots, onions and mushrooms for 5 minutes.

Stir in the flour, mustard and crumbled stock cube and gradually add the milk, stirring until the sauce thickens, boils and is smooth.

Remove from the heat and add the chicken, asparagus, seasoning and cream to the sauce. Pour the mixture into a 1.25 litre (2 pint) pie dish.

Roll out the pastry to the same size as the dish, dampen the rim of the dish and cover with the pastry. Use any trimmings to make decorations for the pie. Brush all over with beaten egg. Bake for 25 minutes until the pastry is golden brown.

Scan the **QR Code** with a smartphone for an ingredients shopping list

Cook's TIPS

To get 450g (1lb) cooked chicken, add a small whole chicken to a pan with 1 onion, carrot and leek, sliced. Cover with water, bring to the boil then cover and simmer for 1 hour or until well cooked. Discard the bones and dice the chicken meat. Strain the stock and freeze in handy sized portions for sauces and casseroles.

This luxurious puff-topped chicken pie from 1987 is sure to become a firm family favourite.

A fabulous Sunday lunch or scrumptious alternative for Christmas Day; this pastry parcel from 2002 is packed full of flavour.

Turkey en Croûte

Serves 8
Time approx. 2½ hours
Per portion: 584 Kcal
36g fat (12g saturated)

Preheat the oven to 200°C/180°fan/Gas 6. Line a 900g (2lb) loaf tin with non-stick baking paper, leaving extra paper overhanging the top of the tin.

Heat the butter in a frying pan, add the onion and fry for 5 minutes until softened. Transfer to a large bowl and add the sausagemeat, zest, cranberries, pine nuts, apricots and sage. Season with salt and pepper then add half the egg and mix together.

Line the base of the loaf tin with one third of the turkey slices then spoon over half the cranberry sauce. Spoon half the sausagemeat mixture on top and press into an even layer. Repeat with another layer of turkey then the rest of the sauce, then the stuffing and top with the last of the turkey. Fold the paper over the top then cover with foil. Bake for 1¼ hours or until the juices run clear when pierced with a skewer. Cool in the tin.

Increase the oven temperature to 220°C/200°C fan/ Gas 7. Roll out the pastry on a floured surface to 40 x 30cm (16 x 12 in). Take the turkey out of the tin and peel off the paper, place on the pastry so that the long edges of the turkey are parallel with the short edges of the pastry. Brush the pastry edges with egg, fold the short edges up and over the turkey to enclose then fold in the ends.

Transfer to an oiled baking sheet, brush with egg and bake for 35-40 minutes until golden. To check it's hot, insert a skewer, hold for 30 seconds then remove – the tip of the skewer should feel hot.

Butter 25g (1oz)

Onion 1 small, peeled and finely chopped

Good-quality herby pork sausages 3, skinned

Orange 1, finely grated zest

Dried cranberries 2 tbsp

Pine nuts 50g (2oz)

Dried ready-to-eat apricots 50g (2oz), chopped

Chopped fresh sage 3 tbsp

Salt and freshly ground black pepper

Egg 1, beaten

Sliced turkey breast 2 x 425g (15oz) packs

Cranberry sauce 2 tbsp

Shortcrust pastry 500g (1lb 2oz)

Plain flour to dust

Cook's TIPS Decorate with pastry leaves, if wished. Check the pastry after about 20 minutes; if it's browning too quickly, cover with foil. Serve hot with all the trimmings for Christmas dinner or cold as part of a buffet.

Scan the **QR Code** with a smartphone for an ingredients shopping list

Roast Pork with Fanned Potatoes & Treacle-Glazed Red Cabbage

Serves 6

Time approx. 2 hours

Per portion: 611 Kcal
17g fat (4.5g saturated)

Loin of pork 1.5kg (3lb 5oz) with bone, chined

Salt 2 tbsp, plus ½ tsp

Vegetable oil 4 tbsp

Baking potatoes 6, peeled and halved

Sage 4 sprigs

Red cabbage 700g (1lb 9oz), trimmed, cored and finely shredded

Red wine vinegar 4 tbsp

Demerara sugar 6 tbsp

Butter 25g (1oz)

Black treacle 1 tbsp

Coarsely ground black pepper

Chopped parsley or chives 1–2 tbsp

Preheat the oven to 230°C/210°fan/Gas 8.

Score the pork skin with a sharp knife and rub all over with 1 tbsp salt. Brush with some oil and rub in another 1 tbsp salt.

Place the pork in a roasting tin and cook for 20 minutes. Reduce the heat to 200°C/180°fan/Gas 6 and roast for a further 1¼ hours or until the juices run clear when the pork is pierced with a knife.

Meanwhile, cut the potatoes across at 5mm (¼in) intervals, making sure not to cut all the way through. Place in cold water and leave for 10 minutes.

Drain the potatoes and place in another roasting tin with the sage. Pour over 3 tablespoons of oil. Roast for 1½ hours until tender and crisp.

Meanwhile, put the cabbage, vinegar, sugar and 1 tsp salt into a non-aluminium saucepan. Add 225ml (8fl oz) water, cover and cook gently for about 1 hour until the cabbage is tender.

Drain the cabbage well then return to the pan and mix in the butter and treacle. Season with pepper and serve sprinkled with parsley or chives.

Leave the pork to rest in a warm place for 10 minutes before carving. Serve with the potatoes and red cabbage.

Scan the **QR Code** with a smartphone for an ingredients shopping list

Cook's TIPS

Make the most of baby pickling onions or shallots when in season and add 12 peeled shallots to the potato roasting tin for the last 30 minutes of cooking.

Serve this gorgeous roast pork with fanned potatoes from 2000 with the rich and flavourful cabbage from 2004 – the perfect roast dinner for family or friends.

Tender pork and vegetables topped with a crunchy cheesy crumble make this meal from the 1991 Dairy Diary a real treat.

Pork Crumble

Serves 4
Time 1 hour
Per portion: 524 Kcal
23g fat (12g saturated)

Preheat the oven to 200°C/180°fan/Gas 6.

Dry-fry the pork in a large pan until browned. Add 25g (1oz) of the flour and cook for 2–3 minutes, then gradually stir in the milk. Season with salt and pepper and simmer for 5 minutes.

Add the sage, leeks and mushrooms to the sauce and cook for 10 minutes.

Meanwhile, put the remaining flour into a bowl with the mustard, paprika and some pepper and rub in the butter until the mixture resembles breadcrumbs. Stir in the cheese, parsley and oats.

Pour the pork mixture into a 900ml (1½ pint) ovenproof dish. Sprinkle the crumble mixture on top and bake for 25 minutes. Serve the crumble hot with peas, if wished.

Lean pork 450g (1lb), diced

Plain flour 150g (5oz)

Milk 450ml (¾ pint)

Salt and freshly ground black pepper

Chopped sage 2 tsp

Leeks 4, washed and sliced

Mushrooms 110g (4oz), sliced

Mustard powder 1 tsp

Paprika 1 tsp

Butter 50g (2oz)

Cheddar cheese 50g (2oz), grated

Chopped parsley 2 tbsp

Porridge oats 25g (1oz)

Peas to serve (optional)

Scan the **QR Code** with a smartphone for an ingredients shopping list

Cook's TIPS
For those who are partial to the odd glass of cider, why not add 150ml (¼ pint) in place of the same amount of milk. It's good way to use up flat cider.

Serves 6

Time 50 minutes

Per portion: 495 Kcal
28g fat (13g saturated)

Sausage & Leek Supper

Potatoes 700g (1lb 9oz), peeled and sliced

Butter 25g (1oz)

Sausages with herbs 450g (1lb), sliced

Onion 1, peeled and sliced

Leeks 4, washed and sliced

Plain flour 40g (1½oz)

Milk 450ml (¾ pint)

Smoked Cheddar cheese 110g (4oz), grated

Fresh breadcrumbs 25g (1oz)

Roast baby vegetables to serve (optional)

Preheat the oven to 200°C/180°fan/Gas 6.

Cook the potatoes in boiling salted water for 4-5 minutes until just tender. Drain.

Meanwhile, melt the butter in a large pan, add the sausage slices and cook for 5 minutes. Add the onion and leeks and cook for a further 5 minutes.

Add the flour, cook for 1 minute, then gradually add the milk and 75g (3oz) of the cheese, stirring. Bring to the boil then simmer for 1–2 minutes, stirring continuously.

Transfer to a 2 litre (3½ pint) ovenproof dish, arrange the potato slices on top, sprinkle with the breadcrumbs and the remaining cheese and bake for 20-30 minutes until browned. Serve hot with roast vegetables, if you like.

Scan the
QR Code with a smartphone for an ingredients shopping list

Cook's
TIPS

Keep an eye on the potato slices as you cook them in boiling water; you want them to be only just tender as they will also cook when the dish goes into the oven. Otherwise they will be tricky to arrange on the top.

A perennial favourite with many readers, this comforting Sausage & Leek Supper from 1991 is perfect to place on the table and share.

Puffed and golden Yorkshire filled with sausage and apple – who couldn't love this homely dish from the 1993 Dairy Diary?

Sausagemeat Yorkshire

Serves 4
Time 1¼ hours
Per portion: 586 Kcal
39g fat (14g saturated)

Preheat the oven to 220°C/200°fan/Gas 7. Brush an 18 x 25cm (7 x 10in) roasting tin with oil and place in the oven to heat for 5 minutes.

Mix the sausagemeat, onion and cheese together. Form into eight small burger shapes.

Heat the oil in a large frying pan and fry the 'burgers' for 3–4 minutes on each side. Transfer to the greased dish and top with apple slices.

Sift the flour and salt together. Gradually beat in the egg and milk until smooth, then pour into the dish. Bake for 40–45 minutes until browned and crisp. Serve immediately with your chosen vegetables and plenty of gravy.

Olive oil to brush
Sausagemeat 500g (1lb 2oz)
Onion 1, peeled and chopped
Cheddar cheese 50g (2oz), grated
Vegetable oil 1 tbsp
Green dessert apple 1, cored, sliced and halved
Plain flour 110g (4oz)
Salt a pinch
Egg 1, lightly beaten
Milk 225ml (8fl oz)
Gravy and a selection of vegetables to serve (optional)

Scan the **QR Code** with a smartphone for an ingredients shopping list

The secret of really good Yorkshires is to make sure that the roasting tin is hot when you add the batter – it should sizzle instantly as it hits the tin.

Serves 6

Time 1½ hours

Per portion: 429 Kcal
30g fat (13g saturated)

Lamb Crown Roast

Racks of lamb 2, with 6–8 cutlets each

Butter 50g (2oz)

Onion 1 large, peeled and chopped

Garlic 2 cloves, peeled and crushed

Celery 3 sticks, sliced

Dried apricots 50g (2oz), chopped

Dried cherries 50g (2oz), chopped

Pistachio nuts 50g (2oz), chopped

Fresh breadcrumbs 110g (4oz)

Chopped mint 3 tbsp

Lemon 1, grated zest and juice

Egg 1, beaten

Salt and freshly ground black pepper

Steamed new potatoes and vegetables to serve (optional)

Preheat the oven to 200°C/180°fan/Gas 6.

Bend the racks to form a crown, fat side inward, and secure with string.

Melt the butter in a pan and fry the onion, garlic and celery for about 5 minutes until softened. Stir in the chopped apricots, cherries, pistachios, breadcrumbs, mint, lemon zest and juice, egg and seasoning. Leave to cool slightly, then fill the crown centre.

Weigh the filled crown, then transfer to a roasting tin, cover with foil and roast, allowing 15 minutes per 450g (1lb), plus 15 minutes. Leave to rest for 5 minutes before carving. Serve with new potatoes and a selection of vegetables, if you like.

Scan the **QR Code** with a smartphone for an ingredients shopping list

Cook's
TIPS

To make gravy, transfer the lamb to a warm plate and keep hot. Pour off any fat to leave the juices then stir in 2 tbsp plain flour, cook briefly then stir in 300ml (½ pint) lamb stock, 150ml (¼ pint) dry white wine and 1 tsp Dijon mustard. Season, bring to the boil and cook for 2 minutes then strain into a gravy boat and serve.

This show-stopper from the 2002 Dairy Diary uses a mixture of succulent fruits to stuff a lamb crown – providing an impressive platter for the centre of any dinner table.

*Feel-good food doesn't come much better
than this lamb pie from the 2006 Diary –
serve simply with a spoonful of creamy mash.*

Minced Lamb Pie

Serves 6
Time 1½ hours
Per portion: 618 Kcal
41g fat (17g saturated)

Heat the butter and oil in a frying pan, add the onion and carrot and cook until softened. Add the lamb and cook until browned all over. Stir in the flour then add the stock, rosemary, tomato purée, Worcestershire sauce, sherry, if using, and seasoning. Cover and simmer for 20 minutes, stirring occasionally. Leave to cool.

Preheat the oven to 200°C/180°fan/Gas 6.

Roll out half of the pastry and line a 25cm (10in) enamel pie plate. Fill with the lamb mixture.

Roll out the remaining pastry until large enough to cover the pie. Brush the edge of the pastry in the tin with water, cover with the rolled-out pastry and press the edges together to seal. Trim and decorate the edge, brush with egg and make a small hole in the centre.

Place on a baking tray and bake for 20 minutes. Sprinkle with the cheese and bake for a further 15–20 minutes until the pastry is golden. Serve with mash and steamed green beans, if you like.

Butter 25g (1oz)

Olive oil 1 tbsp

Onion 1 large, peeled and chopped

Carrot 1 large, peeled and finely diced

Minced lamb 500g (1lb 2oz)

Plain flour 2 tbsp

Lamb or chicken stock 150ml (¼ pint)

Chopped rosemary 4 tsp or 2 tsp dried

Tomato purée 4 tsp

Worcestershire sauce 1 tbsp

Sherry 2 tbsp (optional)

Salt and freshly ground black pepper

Shortcrust pastry 400g (14oz)

Egg 1, beaten

Cheddar cheese 50g (2oz), grated

Mash and green beans to serve (optional)

Cook's TIPS

If you don't have an enamel pie plate then line a 23cm (9in) shallow loose bottomed tart tin with half the pastry, add the filling and roll out the remaining pastry to just a little bigger than the top of the tin then press the pastry edges together and trim off the excess before glazing and topping with cheese.

Scan the **QR Code** with a smartphone for an ingredients shopping list

Serves 4

Time 20 minutes

Per portion: 363 Kcal
23g fat (13g saturated)

Boeuf Stroganoff

Butter 50g (2oz)

Onion 1, peeled and sliced

Button mushrooms 110g (4oz), sliced

Dijon mustard 2 tsp

Plain flour 2 tbsp

Soured cream 150ml (¼ pint)

Rump steak 450g (1lb), trimmed and cut into strips

Salt and freshly ground black pepper

Lemon juice 1 tsp

Paprika to dust

Chopped parsley 2 tbsp

Cooked rice and lemon wedges to serve (optional)

Melt half the butter in a pan and sauté the onion and mushrooms for about 5 minutes until softened. Stir in the mustard and flour, then gradually blend in the soured cream.

Heat the remaining butter in a frying pan and sauté the meat until browned. Stir it into the sauce, season to taste and add the lemon juice. Dust with paprika and sprinkle with parsley. Serve at once with rice and lemon wedges, if you like.

Scan the
QR Code with a smartphone for an ingredients shopping list

Cook's
TIPS

For a decadent open steak sandwich you could spoon the Stroganoff on to lightly toasted sliced sourdough bread and top with rocket or watercress.

*This classic Stroganoff taken from the
1986 Dairy Diary is rich and creamy with a
generous portion of soured cream.*

This stunning dessert from 2005 makes a beautiful alternative to Christmas pudding, or serve anytime as a decadent treat.

Frozen Christmas Pudding

Serves 8

Time 30 minutes plus soaking and freezing

Per portion: 372 Kcal
24g fat (14g saturated)

Soak the fruits with the orange zest, juice and liqueur for 2 hours. Line a 1.5 litre (2½ pint) pudding basin with cling film.

Whisk the cream, vanilla and icing sugar until soft peaks form. Fold in the fruits and spoon into the basin. Cover and freeze.

Put the chocolate, butter and 3 tablespoons of water in a bowl over a pan of barely simmering water, stirring occasionally, until melted and smooth. Leave to cool.

Line a plate with non-stick baking paper. Carefully dip the pudding basin into a bowl of warm water and unmould onto the plate. Remove the cling film and pour the chocolate over to cover. Freeze uncovered, then wrap in cling film and foil and return to the freezer until needed.

Remove from the freezer 25 minutes before serving.

Ready-to-eat dried apricots
65g (2½oz), chopped

Ready-to-eat dried figs
65g (2½oz), chopped

Ready-to-eat dried prunes
75g (3oz), chopped

Maraschino or glacé cherries
65g (2½oz), halved

Orange ½, grated zest plus 3 tbsp juice

Orange liqueur, brandy or sherry 2 tbsp

Double cream 300ml (½ pint)

Vanilla extract 1 tsp

Icing sugar 90g (3½oz)

Dark chocolate 110g (4oz), roughly chopped

Unsalted butter 20g (¾oz)

Cook's TIPS

For a gingered pudding, omit the vanilla extract and stir in 4 tsp finely chopped crystallised or glacé ginger.

Scan the **QR Code** with a smartphone for an ingredients shopping list

Serves 6

Time 50 minutes plus cooling

Per portion: 515 Kcal
37g fat (18g saturated)

Dark chocolate 110g (4oz), chopped

Eggs 4, separated

Caster sugar 110g (4oz), plus extra to sprinkle

Pecan nuts 50g (2oz), chopped

Double cream 250ml (9fl oz)

Maple syrup 4 tbsp

Icing sugar to dust

Chocolate leaves and **cranberries** to decorate (optional)

Chocolate Maple Yule Log

Preheat the oven to 180°C/160°fan/Gas 4. Grease a 33 x 23cm (13 x 9in) Swiss roll tin and line with non-stick baking paper.

Melt the chocolate in a bowl over a pan of barely simmering water.

Whisk the egg yolks and caster sugar together for 15 minutes until thick and pale. Stir in the melted chocolate and pecans.

Whisk the egg whites until stiff and fold into the chocolate mixture. Pour into the tin and bake for 20 minutes until risen and just firm to the touch. Cover with a clean teacloth and leave to cool.

When ready to roll, place the teacloth on the work surface, cover with a sheet of non-stick baking paper, sprinkle with sugar and then turn out the sponge onto the paper. Peel off the lining.

Whip the cream and maple syrup together until stiff then spread over the cooled cake. Roll up from the short end. Dust with icing sugar and decorate with chocolate leaves and cranberries if you like.

Scan the **QR Code** with a smartphone for an ingredients shopping list

Cook's TIPS

The sponge will crack slightly as you roll it and make it look more authentic. You can make chocolate holly leaves by drizzling melted chocolate onto non-stick baking paper. Leave to dry and use to decorate.

This gorgeous maple-infused chocolate log from the 2003 Dairy Diary makes a fantastic Christmas table centrepiece.

Pears pair with chocolate perfectly and in this recipe from 1985 they are also presented on a scrumptious crisp coconut base. Divine.

Chocolate Pear Flan

Serves 6

Time 50 minutes plus cooling

Per portion: 555 Kcal
40g fat (26g saturated)

Preheat the oven to 170°C/150°fan/Gas 3.

Sift 90g (3½oz) of the flour and the drinking chocolate into a bowl. Rub in the butter and stir in the coconut and 50g (2oz) of the sugar then press together gently to form a dough. Press the dough into the base and sides of a 20cm (8in) flan tin. Prick the base and bake for 30 minutes. Cool.

Melt the chocolate in a heatproof bowl set over a pan of barely simmering water.

In a pan, off the heat, beat the egg yolk and the remaining sugar together until thick. Stir in the remaining flour and the milk. Heat, stirring, until the mixture boils and thickens. Simmer for 3 minutes then remove from the heat and stir in the melted chocolate. Cool.

Remove the pastry case from the tin and spread the cold chocolate cream over the pastry. Whip the cream until soft peaks form and then spoon onto the chocolate. Arrange the pear halves on the cream and sprinkle with grated chocolate.

Plain flour 110g (4oz)

Drinking chocolate 25g (1oz)

Butter 110g (4oz)

Desiccated coconut 65g (2½oz)

Caster sugar 75g (3oz)

Dark chocolate 75g (3oz), chopped, plus extra grated to decorate

Egg yolk 1

Milk 150ml (¼ pint)

Double cream 150ml (½ pint)

Pear halves 410g can, drained

Cook's TIPS

The shortbread base and chocolate filling can be prepped in advance but don't add the whipped cream and pears until just as you are about to serve.

Scan the **QR Code** with a smartphone for an ingredients shopping list

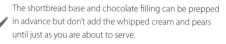

Serves 4–6

Time 1 hour

Per portion: 411 Kcal
17g fat (6.2g saturated)

Shortcrust pastry 250g (9oz)

Eggs 3, separated

Caster sugar 175g (6oz)

Cornflour 2 tbsp

Milk 300ml (½ pint)

Vanilla extract 1 tsp

Bananas 2, sliced

Cinnamon to sprinkle

Single cream to serve
(optional)

Banana Cream Pie

Preheat the oven to 190°C/170°fan/Gas 5.

Roll out the pastry on a lightly floured surface and use it to line an 18cm (7in) flan tin. Line the pastry with non-stick baking paper and fill it with baking beans. Bake blind for 10 minutes. Remove the paper and beans and cook for a further 5 minutes until crisp. Remove from the oven and reduce the temperature to 150°C/130°fan/Gas 2.

In a heatproof bowl, beat the egg yolks with 50g (2oz) of the caster sugar and the cornflour until pale and thick.

Bring the milk to the boil then gradually whisk into the egg mixture. Cook the bowl of custard over a pan of simmering water, stirring continuously until thick. Cool. Stir in the vanilla.

Arrange the banana slices in the pastry case, reserving a few for decoration. Pour the custard over the bananas.

Whisk 2 egg whites until stiff, beat in half the remaining sugar and fold in the rest. Pipe the meringue on top of the custard, leaving the centre uncovered. Bake for 15–20 minutes until the meringue is golden. Leave to cool for 1–2 hours.

Arrange the remaining banana slices in the centre. Sprinkle the bananas with cinnamon and serve cold with cream, if you like.

Scan the
QR Code with a
smartphone for
an ingredients
shopping list

Cook's
TIPS

To prevent the banana used for decoration from going brown keep half a banana in its skin before slicing.

From the 1987 Dairy Diary, this pie has a crisp pastry base filled with banana slices and custard topped with fluffy meringue.

A delicous twist on a classic trifle, this combination of ginger cake and pear with custard and cream, from 2011, is wonderful.

Pear & Ginger Trifle

Serves 6

Time 25 minutes plus cooling

Per portion: 437 Kcal
30g fat (16g saturated)

Put the pears in a pan with the cider and sugar. Simmer for about 10 minutes until the pears are soft, then leave to cool.

Arrange the ginger cake in a glass serving dish and pour the pears and cider over the top. Top with cooled custard and leave to set.

Spoon whipped cream around the edge of the custard and sprinkle with orange and lime zest, if using. Chill for at least 2 hours before serving.

Pears 450g (1lb), peeled, cored and sliced

Cider 150ml (¼ pint)

Soft brown sugar 50g (2oz)

Jamaica ginger cake ½ loaf, sliced

Custard 450ml (¾ pint), cooled

Double cream 250ml (9fl oz), whipped

Orange and lime 1 of each, grated zest to decorate (optional)

Cook's TIPS

For a Jamaican rum trifle, arrange the ginger cake in the base of the dish, drizzle with 4 tbsp dark rum, then top with 4 slices fresh pineapple, diced. Pour over the custard and top with cream and zest as above.

Scan the **QR Code** with a smartphone for an ingredients shopping list

Serves 6

Time 35 minutes

Per portion: 309 Kcal

7.8g fat (2.2g saturated)

Swiss roll 1

Apricot halves 410g can, drained

Custard powder 2 tbsp

Eggs 3, separated

Caster sugar 110g (4oz), plus 1 tbsp

Milk 450ml (¾ pint)

Toasted flaked almonds 25g (1oz) to decorate (optional)

Hot Swiss Trifle

Preheat the oven to 180°C/160°fan/Gas 4.

Slice the Swiss roll and arrange with the apricots in a 1.25 litre (2 pint) ovenproof dish.

Blend the custard powder, egg yolks and 1 tablespoon of the sugar together with a little of the milk. Heat the rest of the milk until nearly boiling, then pour onto the custard mixture and stir well. Return to the pan and bring to the boil, stirring continuously until thick. Pour over the apricots.

Whisk the egg whites until stiff then fold in the remaining caster sugar. Pile the meringue on top of the custard and sprinkle on the almonds, if using. Bake for about 20 minutes until the meringue is golden. Serve hot.

Scan the **QR Code** with a smartphone for an ingredients shopping list

If the trifle isn't being served to children you could drizzle the Swiss roll with 2-3 tbsp sherry or Marsala before topping with the apricots.

Warm and comforting, this scrumptious trifle has a fluffy baked meringue topping and is taken from the very first Dairy Diary in 1982.

There's nothing better than a hot crumble on a cold day and this delicous raspberry version from 1998 has a crunchy oatmeal topping.

Rustic Raspberry Crumble

Serves 4
Time 40–50 minutes
Per portion: 593 Kcal
26g fat (15g saturated)

Preheat the oven to 200°C/180°fan/Gas 6. Toast the oatmeal for 3-4 minutes in a dry non-stick pan until lightly browned. Cool.

Gently stir together the raspberries, apples and brown sugar in a 1.25 litre (2 pint) ovenproof dish.

In a bowl, rub together the butter, flour and oatmeal until the mixture resembles breadcrumbs. Stir in most of the demerara sugar. Spoon the crumble mixture over the fruit and press down lightly. Sprinkle with the remaining demerara sugar and bake for 30–40 minutes until golden brown. Serve hot, with ice cream, custard or cream.

Medium oatmeal 110g (4oz)

Frozen raspberries 350g pack

Cooking apples 450g (1lb), peeled, cored and sliced

Soft light brown sugar 25g (1oz)

Butter 110g (4oz)

Plain flour 110g (4oz)

Demerara sugar 110g (4oz)

Vanilla ice cream, custard or cream to serve

Cook's TIPS
Frozen raspberries make a great freezer standby and are often cheaper than their fresh counterparts. Frozen blackberries or mixed summer fruits could also be used.

Scan the **QR Code** with a smartphone for an ingredients shopping list

Serves 6

Time 50 minutes

Per portion: 467 Kcal
27g fat (13g saturated)

Light muscovado sugar
75g (3oz)

Golden syrup 1 tbsp

Butter 75g (3oz)

Cornflour 1 tbsp

Lemon juice 1 tbsp

Cooking apples 900g (2lb),
peeled, cored and thickly sliced

**Ready-rolled sweet dessert
pastry** 320g pack

Milk to brush

Caster sugar 1 tbsp

Butterscotch Apple Pie

Preheat the oven to 200°C/180°fan/Gas 6.

Put the muscovado sugar, syrup and butter in a
pan and heat gently until the butter has melted and
the sugar has dissolved. Mix the cornflour with the
lemon juice and add to the sauce. Heat, stirring, until
thickened.

Put the apples in a pie dish and pour over the
butterscotch sauce.

Place the pastry on a lightly floured surface and cut
out a lid for the pie and a long strip of pastry about
1cm (½in) wide. Dampen the rim of the pie dish and
put the strip of pastry around it. Dampen the pastry
strip and cover with the pastry lid. Use any trimmings
to make decorations. Make a slit in the top, brush
with milk and sprinkle with caster sugar. Bake for 25-
30 minutes until golden.

Scan the
QR Code with a
smartphone for
an ingredients
shopping list

Cook's
TIPS

Keep stirring the butterscotch sauce as you make it so that
the sauce doesn't stick and catch on the base of the pan.

With a secret butterscotch sauce, this apple pie from the 1999 Diary is a truly delicious pudding to serve after Sunday lunch.

*These tiny Caribbean-inspired fruit
puddings from 2010 are a delicious and easy
alternative to the usual Christmas pudding.*

Calypso Puddings

Makes 8

Time 3½ hours

Per pudding: 348 Kcal
4g fat (0.9g saturated)

Grease eight 200ml (7fl oz) pudding moulds with butter and line the bases with non-stick baking paper. Cut eight larger rounds from baking paper and foil for covering the puddings.

Put all the ingredients into a large bowl. Mix well, then spoon into the moulds and smooth the tops. Place the larger paper rounds on top and cover securely with foil.

Steam the puddings for 2 hours.

When ready to serve, turn the puddings out onto plates and decorate with pineapple slices, if using.

Butter to grease

Ready-to-eat dried prunes 200g (7oz), roughly chopped

Lemon 1, grated zest and juice

Orange 1, grated zest and juice

White or dark rum 4 tbsp

Soft dark brown sugar 50g (2oz)

Eggs 3, beaten

Ready-to-eat dried apricots 110g (4oz), chopped

Raisins 150g (5oz)

Sultanas 150g (5oz)

Fresh mango 110g (4oz), peeled and cut into 1cm (½in) cubes

Fresh pineapple 110g (4oz), peeled and cut into 1cm (½in) cubes, plus extra to serve (optional)

Maraschino cherries 110g (4oz), drained and quartered

Fresh breadcrumbs 200g (7oz)

Scan the
QR Code with a smartphone for an ingredients shopping list

Cook's TIPS

These make a delicious alternative Christmas pudding. They can be prepared and cooked 6–8 weeks ahead and frozen in the moulds. Reheat by defrosting and then steaming for 45 minutes before serving.

Serves 6 for nibbles

Time 40 minutes

Per portion: 149 Kcal
9.9g fat (2g saturated)

Bacon Wraps

Rindless smoked streaky bacon rashers 10–12

Melon 6 x 2.5cm (1in) cubes

Large pimento-stuffed olives 6

Pitted black olives 6

Ready-to-eat dried prunes 6

Sun-dried tomatoes in olive oil 6 x 2.5cm (1in) pieces

Olive oil for brushing

Freshly ground black pepper

Using the back of a knife, stretch the bacon rashers out thinly.

Cutting to fit, wrap a piece of bacon round each piece of melon, olive, prune and sun-dried tomato, securing each one with a wooden cocktail stick. Place on a baking tray, brush with olive oil and season with pepper. Cover and chill until needed.

Preheat the oven to 220°C/200°fan/Gas 7. Cook the bacon wraps for 7–10 minutes until hot and slightly crisp. Serve hot with pre-dinner drinks.

Scan the **QR Code** with a smartphone for an ingredients shopping list

Cook's TIPS

Make in advance and store in the fridge until your guests arrive. Then all you need to do is pop them in the oven before serving. They're particularly good served with chilled Prosecco.

These little parcels of delight from the 2005
Dairy Diary are perfect for serving with
drinks when your guests first arrive.

An easy starter for vegetarians and meat-eaters alike, these crisp mushroom pots from the 1990 Diary are simply delicious.

Mushroom Ramekins

Serves 4 as a starter
Time 40 minutes
Per portion: 539 Kcal
52g fat (29g saturated)

Preheat the oven to 190°C/170°fan/Gas 5. Lightly oil four 175ml (6fl oz) ramekin dishes and place in a roasting tin.

Heat the butter and olive oil in a frying pan, add the onion and mushrooms and fry, stirring, until the onion has softened and the mushrooms are just beginning to turn golden. Divide between the ramekin dishes, sprinkle with half the blue cheese and mix together.

Mix the egg, double cream, thyme and a little salt and pepper in a jug then divide between the ramekin dishes.

Mix the remaining blue cheese with the breadcrumbs then scatter over the top of the mushrooms. Pour hot water into the roasting tin to come halfway up the sides of the dishes then bake, uncovered, for 25-30 minutes until the topping is golden and crisp. Serve warm.

Butter 15g (½oz)

Olive oil 2 tsp

Onion 1 small, peeled and finely chopped

Button mushrooms 225g (8oz), sliced

Blue Cheshire cheese 110g (4oz), rind removed and finely chopped

Egg 1, beaten

Double cream 8 tbsp

Dried thyme large pinch

Salt and freshly ground black pepper

Fresh breadcrumbs 25g (1oz)

Cook's TIPS

If you can't find Blue Cheshire cheese then try with Stilton instead. If you're not a blue cheese fan, substitute with your favourite hard British cheese; grated mature Cheddar or Red Leicester would also taste delicious.

Scan the **QR Code** with a smartphone for an ingredients shopping list

Serves 6 as a starter

Time 30 minutes

Per portion: 306 Kcal
25g fat (15g saturated)

Smoked Salmon & Dill Filo Tarts

Filo pastry 3 sheets from a 270g chilled pack of 6 sheets

Butter 40g (1½oz), melted

Crème fraîche 250ml carton

Chopped fresh dill 2 tbsp, plus sprigs to garnish

Smoked salmon slices 110g (4oz), cut into strips

Cucumber 7cm (2½in) piece, finely diced

Salt and freshly ground black pepper

Preheat the oven to 190°C/170°fan/Gas 5. Lightly grease six 10cm (4in) tart tins.

Unroll the pastry, brush one of the sheets with a little of the butter then cut into 8 squares, each about 11cm (4½in). Add one of the squares of filo to one of the tins, then add 3 more squares, each at a slight angle to the first rather like the spokes of a wheel. Repeat to fill a second tin then brush a second sheet of pastry with butter, cut into squares and so on until you have 6 lined tins.

Bake the tarts for 10-12 minutes until golden brown. Carefully remove from the tins and leave to cool on a wire rack.

To make the filling, add the crème fraîche, dill, smoked salmon and cucumber to a bowl. Season with a little salt and pepper and mix together. Cover and chill until needed.

When ready to serve, transfer the tarts to serving plates, spoon in the filling and garnish with the remaining dill sprigs.

Scan the **QR Code** with a smartphone for an ingredients shopping list

Cook's TIPS

Filo pastry is easy to use but does dry out quickly, so unwrap and unfold the pastry sheets only when you are ready to use. Wrap up the remaining filo in clingfilm, slide back into the box and freeze for another time.

*These crisp and luxurious filo tarts from 2003
can be made in advance to allow you time
with your guests until you're ready to serve.*

The classic starter – this chicken liver pâté, served simply with warm toast and rocket leaves, is taken from the 1984 Dairy Diary.

Chicken Liver Pâté

Serves 6 as a starter

Time 30 minutes plus chilling

Per portion: 218 Kcal
16g fat (9.8g saturated)

Melt the butter in a saucepan and gently fry the onion and garlic for 5 minutes or until softened. Add the chicken livers, bay leaves and thyme. Cover and cook gently for about 10 minutes until the livers are tender and no longer pink.

Remove the bay leaves and spoon the mixture into a food processor or blender. Add the brandy and blend until smooth. Stir in the double cream and season to taste.

Pour into ramekins or a large serving dish and chill for 2–3 hours until firm. Garnish with sliced gherkins, if wished, and serve with lightly toasted French bread and a few rocket leaves, if you like.

Butter 50g (2oz)

Onion 1, peeled and finely chopped

Garlic 1 clove, peeled and crushed

Chicken livers 400g pack, trimmed and chopped

Bay leaves 2

Dried thyme ½ tsp

Brandy 2 tbsp

Double cream 3 tbsp

Salt and freshly ground black pepper

Sliced gherkins to serve (optional)

Toasted French bread and rocket to serve (optional)

Cook's TIPS The tops of the pâté can also be covered with a thin layer of melted butter flecked with chopped chives and tarragon then chilled until set for an attractive finish.

Scan the **QR Code** with a smartphone for an ingredients shopping list

Serves 4 as a starter

Time 1 hour

Per portion: 560 Kcal
38g fat (20g saturated)

Ham & Cheese Soufflé

Butter 25g (1oz), plus extra for greasing

Fresh breadcrumbs 25g (1oz)

Plain flour 25g (1oz)

Milk 150ml (¼ pint)

Salt and freshly ground black pepper

Sweet or hot paprika ½ tsp

Eggs 4 large, separated

Cheddar cheese 110g (4oz), grated, plus extra for sprinkling

Parmesan 25g (1oz), grated, plus extra for sprinkling

Snipped chives 3 tbsp

Ham 150g (5oz), cut into thin strips

Preheat the oven to 190°C/170°fan/Gas 5. Grease a 1-1.2 litre (1½-2 pint) soufflé dish and sprinkle breadcrumbs over the base and sides. Wrap the sides of the dish in double thickness non-stick baking paper to stand 4cm (1½in) above the top of the dish (tie with string).

Melt the butter in a saucepan and add the flour then the milk. Bring to the boil, whisking continuously. Season and add the paprika. Allow to cool a little then beat in the egg yolks. Fold in the cheeses, chives and ham.

In a separate bowl whisk the egg whites until stiff, then gently fold into the sauce. Pour the soufflé mixture into the prepared dish and sprinkle with extra cheese.

Place the dish on a baking tray and bake for 35-40 minutes until well risen, golden brown and feels firm but springy to the touch. Serve immediately (remove the paper at the table).

Scan the **QR Code** with a smartphone for an ingredients shopping list

Cook's
TIPS

A soufflé always looks spectacular when taken out of the oven but they quickly lose volume so get your diners sitting at the table before you take it out of the oven. Adding a paper collar around the edge of the dish helps keep the height and stops the soufflé mixture over-spilling the dish during cooking.

An impressive dish to serve at the table,
this rich and creamy ham soufflé, from 2011,
will delight your dinner guests.

*From the 2013 Dairy Diary this dish combines
simple ingredients for maximum flavour.*

Hollandaise Salmon

Serves 4

Time 30 minutes

Calories 688 per portion
61g fat (30g saturated)

Preheat the oven to 150°C/130°fan/Gas 2.

Melt 25g (1oz) of the butter in a pan and then brush onto 4 pieces of foil. Place a salmon fillet on each. Add a lemon slice and season with freshly ground black pepper. Wrap loosely and bake for about 15 minutes, until just cooked.

Meanwhile, to make the sauce, whisk the egg yolks, sugar, vinegar and lemon juice with 1 tbsp water in a bowl set over a pan of simmering water, until the mixture is smooth and leaves a trail on the surface.

Remove the sauce from the heat and whisk in the remaining butter, a few pieces at a time. Season to taste and pour into a jug.

Serve the salmon with the warm sauce, new potatoes, green beans and mangetout, if you like.

Butter 200g (7oz), diced

Salmon fillets 4

Lemon 1, sliced

Salt and freshly ground black pepper

Egg yolks 3

Caster sugar 1 tsp

White wine vinegar 1 tbsp

Lemon juice 1 tbsp

Steamed new potatoes, green beans and mangetout to serve (optional)

Cook's TIPS

Be patient when making the sauce – it may take a while. Whisk continuously until it thickens.

Scan the **QR Code** with a smartphone for an ingredients shopping list

Pesto Chicken with Roasted Potatoes

Potatoes 800g (1¾lb), peeled and cubed

Olive oil 8 tbsp

Walnuts 15g (½oz), chopped

Flat-leaved parsley 50g (2oz), stalks removed

Garlic 1 clove, peeled and chopped

Grated Parmesan cheese 3 tbsp

Salt and freshly ground black pepper

Chicken breasts 4, cut into strips

Crème fraîche 4 tbsp

Watercress to serve (optional)

Preheat the oven to 200°C/180°fan/Gas 6 and heat a roasting tin.

Boil the potatoes for 5 minutes then drain well. Place in the tin with 2 tablespoons of the oil and roast for 40 minutes, turning a few times, until golden and cooked through.

Meanwhile, make the pesto. Dry-fry the walnuts in a frying pan until toasted. Place in a food processor with the parsley, garlic and Parmesan and season with salt. Add 5 tbsp olive oil and whizz to a chunky texture.

Pour the remaining oil into the frying pan and cook the chicken for around 5 minutes until browned. Add the crème fraîche and 3 tbsp pesto and simmer for 5 minutes. Add 2 tbsp more of pesto then serve with the roasted potatoes and watercress, if using.

Scan the
QR Code with a
smartphone for
an ingredients
shopping list

Cook's
TIPS

The pesto sauce can also be stirred through just cooked tagliatelle for a speedy meat-free supper.

This creamy pesto chicken from 2013, served with tiny roasted potatoes, will be a real treat for your dinner guests.

Pork tenderloin, wrapped in Parma ham and
stuffed with Stilton, is served with apples in a
creamy sauce from the 1986 Dairy Diary.

Stuffed Pork Fillet

Serves 4

Time 1 hour

Per portion: 554 Kcal
36g fat (22g saturated)

Preheat the oven to 180°C/160°fan/Gas 4.

Cut the tenderloin into four pieces, then beat into thin escalopes. Spread with the Stilton, add a sage leaf and roll up in a slice of Parma ham.

Heat the butter in a frying pan and fry the pork parcels for 3-5 minutes, until lightly browned. Remove to a plate. Add the onion to the pan and fry gently for around 5 minutes until softened. Stir in the flour, then add the wine, stock and apples. Season and transfer to a casserole dish.

Add the pork parcels to the casserole in a single layer then bake, uncovered, for 35-40 minutes, or until the juices run clear when the pork is pierced with a knife. Cover with foil after 20 minutes if the pork is browning too quickly.

Transfer the pork parcels to serving plates, stir the crème fraîche into the casserole then spoon the sauce around the pork. Serve at once with sauté potatoes and green beans, if you like.

Pork tenderloin 450g (1lb)

Stilton cheese 110g (4oz), at room temperature

Sage 4 leaves

Parma ham 4 slices

Butter 25g (1oz)

Onion 1, peeled and sliced

Plain flour 2 tbsp

Dry white wine 100ml (3½fl oz)

Chicken stock 100ml (3½fl oz)

Dessert apples 2, peeled, cored and diced

Salt and freshly ground black pepper

Crème fraîche 150ml (¼ pint)

Sauté potatoes and green beans to serve (optional)

Cook's TIPS

Prepare the stuffed pork fillet earlier in the day then cover with cling film and chill in the fridge until ready to cook.

Scan the **QR Code** with a smartphone for an ingredients shopping list

Serves 4

Time 1 hour plus proving

Per portion: 1000 Kcal
43g fat (19g saturated)

Kofta Curry with Naan Bread

For the naan bread

Strong white flour 450g (1lb), sifted

Salt ½ tsp

Baking powder 1 tsp

Sugar 1 tsp

Dried yeast 1½ tsp

Egg 1, beaten

Natural yogurt 4 tbsp

Butter 50g (2oz), melted

Warm milk 200ml (7fl oz)

For the curry

Minced lamb 450g (1lb)

Onion 1, peeled and finely chopped

Root ginger 1cm (½in) piece, peeled and grated

Garlic 2 cloves, peeled and crushed

Green chilli 1, deseeded and finely chopped

Chopped coriander 2 tbsp

Egg 1, beaten

Butter 15g (½oz)

Ground coriander 2 tsp

Ground cumin 1 tsp

Ground turmeric ½ tsp

Ground cinnamon ½ tsp

Milk 450ml (¾ pint)

Tomato purée 1 tbsp

Blanched almonds 50g (2oz)

Natural yogurt 150g (5oz)

To make the naan bread, add the flour, salt, baking powder and sugar to a mixing bowl or electric mixer fitted with a dough hook. Add the yeast and mix together.

Add the egg, yogurt and half the butter then gradually add enough warm milk to make a soft but not sticky dough. Knead until smooth, cover and leave in a warm place for an hour or so until doubled in size.

Knead for a minute, then divide into eight balls. Flatten and roll the balls into teardrop shapes. Leave to rest while making the curry.

Mix together the meat, half the onion, and the ginger, garlic, chilli, fresh coriander and egg. Make 24 balls.

Melt the butter in a frying pan and fry the meatballs in batches until evenly browned. Remove from the pan and drain off excess fat from the pan.

Put the remaining onion into the pan and fry gently for 5 minutes until softened. Add the spices and cook for 1 minute, stirring. Add the milk and purée and bring to the boil. Return the meatballs to the pan, cover and simmer for 30 minutes.

Preheat the grill to hot. Add the almonds to the curry and gradually stir in the yogurt – do not boil.

Brush the dough with the remaining butter and grill for 2 minutes each side. Serve with the curry.

Cooking the naan bread under the grill for just a few minutes might seem quick but it really does work. Don't get the bread too close to the heat - about 5cm (2in) distance should be just right.

This mild lamb curry served with homemade naan bread, from the 1987 Dairy Diary, is perfect for an informal evening with friends.

*A decadent treat from the 2005 Dairy Diary –
fillet steaks with olives, anchovies and herbs,
wrapped in a gorgeous crisp puff pastry.*

Mediterranean Steak en Croûte

Serves 4
Time 50 minutes
Per portion: 886 Kcal
65g fat (28g saturated)

Preheat the oven to 220°C/200°fan/Gas 7.

In a shallow dish, coat the steaks with the oil.

Combine the butter with the olives, anchovies, parsley, chives and tomatoes. Season with pepper.

On a lightly floured surface, roll out the pastry to about 3mm (⅛in) thick. Using a saucer as a guide, cut out eight discs 14cm (5½in) in diameter. You will need to re-roll the pastry trimmings. Place four discs on a baking tray, put a steak on each and top with the savoury butter.

Brush the pastry around the steaks with egg and cover with the remaining pastry discs, pressing well to seal. Slash with a knife then brush the tops with egg and bake for 20 minutes until well risen, crisp and golden. Serve hot with buttered new potatoes, and green vegetables, if you like.

Fillet steaks 4, each approx. 9cm (3½in) in diameter

Olive oil 2 tbsp

Butter 50g (2oz), softened

Stuffed green olives 4, chopped

Anchovy fillets 2–3, chopped

Chopped parsley 2 tbsp

Snipped chives 2 tbsp

Sun-dried tomatoes 4, chopped

Freshly ground black pepper

Puff pastry 500g (1lb 2oz)

Egg 1, beaten

New potatoes, asparagus and green beans to serve (optional)

Cook's TIPS

Unlike when making a large beef en croûte, these individual sized pieces of meat do not need frying or sealing first.

Serves 4

Time 20 minutes

Per portion: 510 Kcal
37g fat (24g saturated)

Garlic 1 clove, peeled and crushed

Dry white wine 225ml (8fl oz)

Mature Cheddar cheese 225g (8oz), grated

Lancashire cheese 225g (8oz), grated

Lemon juice 1 tsp

Cornflour 4 tsp

Kirsch 2 tbsp

Bread cubes and vegetable crudités to serve

Two-Cheese Fondue

Rub the inside of the fondue pot with garlic. Add the wine and heat until warm. Add the Cheddar and Lancashire cheeses to the pot with the lemon juice. Cook over a medium heat, stirring all the time, until the cheese melts and just begins to bubble. Remove from the heat.

Blend the cornflour with the kirsch and stir into the cheese mixture. Return to the heat and cook, stirring, until the mixture comes to the boil. Transfer to the spirit stove and serve immediately with vegetable sticks and bread cubes.

Serves 4

Time 10 minutes

Per portion: 375 Kcal
24g fat (15g saturated)

Milk chocolate 225g (8oz)

Single cream 125ml (4fl oz)

Coffee liqueur such as Tia Maria 1–2 tbsp

Fruit and marshmallows to serve

Chocolate Fondue

Grate the chocolate into the fondue pot. Add the cream and coffee liqueur. Heat gently, stirring continuously until the chocolate has melted – do not allow to boil.

Transfer to the spirit stove but do not allow it to get too hot or the chocolate will stiffen. A night light in a holder would be adequate. Serve with a selection of fruit and marshmallows.

Scan the **QR Code** with a smartphone for an ingredients shopping list

Cook's TIPS

For additional dippers for a cheese fondue try with chunks of apple, radishes, halved cherry tomatoes or cauliflower florets.

A savoury fondue
followed by a delicious
chocolate fondue from the
1995 Diary makes for a
convivial evening with friends.

A fluffy, creamy chocolate and coffee ice cream from 1986, which can be made in advance and served when your guests are ready.

Iced Mocha Soufflé

Serves 4

Time 10 minutes plus cooling and freezing

Per portion: 400 Kcal
25g fat (15g saturated)

Put the coffee granules and milk into a pan and heat slowly until boiling. Remove from the heat, add the chopped dark chocolate and stir until melted. Leave to cool.

In a clean bowl whisk the egg whites until stiff then gradually whisk in the sugar, a teaspoon at a time, until thick and glossy.

Fold the whipped cream into the chocolate mixture, then fold in the egg white.

Pour into a plastic box, cover and freeze for 4–6 hours until firm.

Coffee granules 4 tsp

Milk 300ml (½ pint)

Dark chocolate 50g (2oz), chopped

Egg whites 2

Caster sugar 110g (4oz)

Double cream 150ml (¼ pint), whipped

Scan the
QR Code with a smartphone for an ingredients shopping list

Transform this into the Italian dessert *affogato* by placing a scoops of ice cream into cups and pouring some freshly made filter coffee over the top.

Serves 8

Time 25 minutes plus chilling

Per portion: 417 Kcal
26g fat (16g saturated)

Raspberry Amaretto Trifle

Trifle sponges 8 (160g packet)

Raspberry jam 4 tbsp

Amaretto liqueur 150ml (¼ pint)

Ground almonds 110g (4oz)

Amaretti biscuits 50g (2oz), crumbled

Frozen raspberries 350g pack, defrosted at room temperature

Double cream 300ml (½ pint)

Ready-made custard 300ml (½ pint)

Slice the trifle sponges in half and sandwich them together with the jam. Cut each into four and arrange in a trifle dish.

Pour over all but 1 tablespoon of the Amaretto. Sprinkle with 75g (3oz) of the ground almonds and the crumbled amaretti biscuits (reserve a couple for decoration). Reserve a few raspberries for decoration and put the remainder in the dish.

Stir the remaining Amaretto, ground almonds and 3 tablespoons of the cream into the custard. Pour over the raspberries.

Whip the remaining cream until soft peaks form then spread over the custard. Decorate with the reserved raspberries and crumbled biscuits. Chill for at least 2 hours until ready to serve.

Scan the **QR Code** with a smartphone for an ingredients shopping list

Cook's TIPS

If you don't have any amaretto then add a little dry sherry, Marsala or a few tablespoons of Grand Marnier.

This rich, almondy trifle from 1985 will delight your guests with its combination of flavours. It's a real crowd-pleaser.

*From the 2016, this white chocolate cheesecake,
paired perfectly with a sharp cranberry sauce,
will have all your friends asking for the recipe.*

White Chocolate Cheesecake

Serves 8–10

Time 45 minutes plus chilling

Per portion: 678 Kcal
51g fat (31g saturated)

Mix together the butter and crushed biscuits. Press into the base of a 20cm (8in) round loose-based tin. Chill for 10 minutes to firm.

Put the chocolate in a heatproof bowl. Heat the cream in a saucepan until almost simmering then pour over the chocolate. Stir well until the chocolate has melted. Leave to cool.

Beat the cream cheese until soft. Fold into the chocolate cream and mix well. Spoon over the biscuit base and smooth the surface. Cover with cling film and chill for 8 hours or preferably overnight, until set.

Put the cranberries, sugar and orange juice in a saucepan and heat gently, stirring until the sugar has dissolved. Bring slowly to the boil, then simmer for 5–10 minutes.

Remove 12 cranberries and reserve for decoration, then blend the rest until smooth.

Carefully unmould the cheesecake onto a plate. Decorate with the reserved cranberries and white chocolate shavings and then serve with the cranberry coulis.

Butter 75g (3oz), melted

Ginger nut biscuits 200g (7oz), crushed

Good-quality white chocolate 350g (12oz), chopped, plus extra, shaved, to decorate

Double cream 150ml (¼ pint)

Full-fat cream cheese 500g (1lb 2oz)

Frozen cranberries 150g (5oz)

Caster sugar 125g (4½oz)

Orange juice 125ml (4fl oz)

For a summer version of this party dessert, top with fresh strawberries and blueberries and serve with puréed strawberries for an easy no-bake sauce that doesn't need any sugar or added extras.

Scan the **QR Code** with a smartphone for an ingredients shopping list

Serves 8

Time 40 minutes plus cooling

Per portion: 356 Kcal
25g fat (14g saturated)

Ready-rolled puff pastry
320g pack

Icing sugar 50g (2oz), plus 1
tbsp, plus extra to dust

Mascarpone 250g (9oz)

Fromage frais 200g (7oz)

Lemon 1, grated zest and juice

Strawberries 450g (1lb)

Caster sugar 25g (1oz)

Strawberry Puffs

Preheat the oven to 220°C/200°fan/Gas 7. Lightly grease a baking sheet.

Roll out the pastry to about 36 x 23cm (14 x 9in), then sprinkle with 1 tablespoon of icing sugar. Cut into 16 equal-size rectangles. Place on the baking sheet and bake for 10-15 minutes until risen and golden. Cut into two lengthways and leave to cool.

Mix together the mascarpone, fromage frais, 50g (2oz) icing sugar and the lemon zest. Chop one third of the strawberries and stir into the mascarpone.

Put the remaining strawberries in a food processor with the caster sugar and lemon juice and whizz to a purée, then sieve.

Sandwich four pastries with three layers of the mascarpone mixture. Repeat to make eight puffs. Drizzle each serving plate with the strawberry coulis, add a strawberry puff, dust with icing sugar and serve immediately.

Scan the
QR Code with a
smartphone for
an ingredients
shopping list

Cook's
TIPS

Vary the fruits depending on what's in season; autumn blackberries with a little chopped fresh mint, or forced rhubarb mixed with frozen strawberries in early spring.

*Light puff pastry filled with strawberries and creamy
mascarpone, drizzled with strawberry coulis –
a summery treat from the 2002 Dairy Diary.*

Sometimes, the simple things in life are the best – this quick brûlée from 1990 needs only four ingredients, but tastes wonderful.

Easy Fruit Brûlée

Serves 4

Time 15 minutes plus chilling

Per portion: 365 Kcal
28g fat (17g saturated)

Place the fruit in a flameproof dish.

Whip the cream until softly stiff, then fold in the yogurt. Spread over the fruit and chill for 2 hours.

Preheat the grill to hot. Sprinkle the demerara sugar over the cream and place under the grill for a few minutes until the sugar melts and caramelises. Serve hot or cold.

Mixed summer fruits
350g (12oz)

Double cream 200ml (7fl oz)

Natural yogurt 200g (7oz)

Demerara sugar 65g (2½oz)

Cook's TIPS Instead of grilling you could use a cook's blowtorch. Make sure that the dishes that you use are heatproof, especially if grilling.

Scan the **QR Code** with a smartphone for an ingredients shopping list

Serves 6

Time 40 minutes

Per portion: 387 Kcal
6g fat (2.3g saturated)

Eggs 4, separated

Caster sugar 200g (7oz)

Raspberry jam 6 tbsp

Fresh breadcrumbs 6 tbsp

Ready-made custard 425g
carton

Queen of Puddings

Preheat the oven to 180°C/160°fan/Gas 4.

Whisk the egg whites until stiff, then gradually whisk in the sugar until smooth and glossy.

Spoon 1 tablespoon of jam into each of six 250ml (9fl oz) ramekins. Spoon over the breadcrumbs.

Mix two of the egg yolks with the custard then divide among the ramekins. Top with the meringue and bake for 20 minutes until golden.

Scan the
QR Code with a
smartphone for
an ingredients
shopping list

Cook's
TIPS

With the 2 leftover yolks make an easy egg custard by whisking with milk, orange zest and 1-2 tsp caster sugar. Pour into a ramekin and bake in the oven for about 20 minutes until set.

Pretty, simple, and delicious, there's several good reasons why these queen of puddings from the 2001 Dairy Diary are so popular.

A light lemon sponge with a secret lemon sauce, these mini puddings from the 1996 Dairy Diary are perfect to finish a meal on a summer's evening.

Double Lemon Puddings

Serves 4

Time 30 minutes

Per portion: 539 Kcal
27g fat (15g saturated)

Preheat the oven to 190°C/170°fan/Gas 5. Lightly grease four 175ml (6fl oz) ramekins.

Beat together the lemon curd and half the lemon juice and spoon into the ramekins.

Put half the lemon zest and the rest of the lemon juice with the butter, caster sugar, eggs and flour into a mixing bowl or food processor and mix well. Divide the mixture among the ramekins (do not fill right to the top as the mixture will rise) and bake for 20 minutes until risen and golden.

Leave for a few minutes before serving, as the lemon curd will be very hot! Serve with a dusting of icing sugar and the remaining lemon zest.

Lemon curd 5 tbsp

Lemons 2, grated zest and juice

Butter 110g (4oz), softened

Caster sugar 110g (4oz)

Eggs 2, lightly beaten

Self-raising flour 110g (4oz)

Icing sugar to dust

Lemon puddle pudding but made with the easiest sauce ever – what could be simpler than stirring extra lemon juice into lemon curd?

Cook's TIPS

Scan the **QR Code** with a smartphone for an ingredients shopping list

Makes 1 loaf

Time 45 minutes

Per slice: 140 Kcal

Fat 2g (1.2g saturated)

Plain flour 450g (1lb)

Irish porridge oats with multi seeds 50g (2oz)

Salt 1 tsp

Bicarbonate of soda 1 tsp

Butter or white fat 25g (1oz)

Finely chopped fresh rosemary 2 tbsp

Fresh cultured buttermilk 300ml pot

Whole milk 100ml (3½fl oz)

Irish Soda Bread

Preheat the oven to 200°C/180°fan/Gas 6.

Mix together the flour, oats, salt and bicarbonate of soda. Add the butter or fat and rub in until it resembles fine crumbs. Stir in the rosemary.

Add the buttermilk and enough milk so that you can knead to make a soft but not sticky dough.

Transfer to a greased and floured baking sheet and shape into an 18cm (7in) round. Score into four and bake for 30-40 minutes or until golden and sounds hollow when tapped on the base.

Serve warm with soup or a selection of cheeses or meats and pickles.

Scan the **QR Code** with a smartphone for an ingredients shopping list

Cook's TIPS

You can buy packets of Irish porridge oats mixed with sunflower, flax, pumpkins and hemp seeds but if you can't find them use plain Irish porridge oats instead. Wrap in a teacloth when you take it out of the oven for a soft crust, or omit the cloth if you prefer a crisper crust.

A really quick and easy loaf flavoured with rosemary, this soda bread from 2014 is the perfect bake for when you're in a hurry.

These fluffy muffins from 2007, flavoured with bacon and chives and served with a tomato butter, a[re] perfect for elevenses when you fancy a savoury fix.

Savoury Muffins

Makes 8
Time 40 minutes
Per muffin: 351 Kcal
22g fat (11g saturated)

In a dry frying pan, gently fry the bacon until lightly browned and crisp. Leave to cool.

Preheat the oven to 220°C/200°fan/Gas 7. Line a muffin tray with muffin cases.

Sift the cornmeal, flour and baking powder into a mixing bowl, mix in 2 tablespoons of chives and the bacon, then make a well in the centre.

Melt 75g (3oz) of the butter, mix with the eggs and milk, then pour into the flour. Mix gently, then spoon into the muffin cases and bake for 15–20 minutes until well risen, lightly browned and springy to touch.

Meanwhile, blend the remaining butter with the tomatoes and the remaining chives. Serve with the warm muffins.

Rindless streaky bacon rashers 175g (6oz), chopped
Fine cornmeal 110g (4oz)
Plain flour 175g (6oz)
Baking powder 1 tbsp
Finely snipped chives 3 tbsp
Butter 150g (5oz)
Eggs 2, beaten
Milk 225ml (8fl oz)
Sun-dried tomatoes 40g (1½oz), finely chopped

Cook's TIPS
Unlike other bakes, muffins need only the minimum of mixing to get a light fluffy texture. Too much stirring and they will be heavy.

Scan the **QR Code** with a smartphone for an ingredients shopping list

Makes 18

Time 40 mins plus cooling

Per biscuit: 102 Kcal

Fat 2g (1.5g is saturated)

Dainty Iced Gingerbread

Plain flour 150g (5oz)

Ground ginger 1 tsp

Ground mixed spice ½ tsp

Butter 50g (2oz)

Soft light muscovado sugar 50g (2oz)

Milk 1 tbsp

Golden syrup 2 tbsp

Royal icing sugar 150g (5oz)

Edible silver sugar balls to decorate

In a mixing bowl stir together the flour, ginger and mixed spice.

Put the butter, muscovado sugar, milk and golden syrup in a pan. Set over low heat and stir gently until it has completely melted and is smooth. Leave to cool for a couple of minutes.

Pour the butter mixture into the flour mixture. Mix well to make a dough. Leave until cool enough to handle, then gently knead to make a neat ball.

Preheat the oven to 180°C/160°fan/Gas 4.

Roll out the dough on a lightly floured surface and stamp out 18 hearts and/or stars, measuring about 5cm (2in). Re-roll the trimmings as necessary. Transfer to baking sheets lined with non-stick baking paper and bake for 10-12 minutes.

Leave the biscuits to firm, then transfer to a wire rack to finish cooling.

Make the icing according to the packet's instructions. Spoon into a piping bag and pipe squiggles, dots and stripes onto the biscuits. Decorate with edible silver balls. Leave to set.

Scan the **QR Code** with a smartphone for an ingredients shopping list

Cook's TIPS

These needn't be just for Christmas; cut out small gingerbread men and ladies, letters of the alphabet or numbers with biscuit cutters and leave plain or pipe on icing and sprinkle with small sweets.

Cute mini gingerbread, decorated with icing and tiny silver balls from the 2014 Dairy Diary – the perfect gift when visiting friends.

Crunchy and utterly moreish, this nutty brittle from the 2014 Diary, is wonderful served with a hot cup of coffee.

Crunchy Peanut Brittle

Makes 425g (15oz)
Time 25 minutes plus cooling
Per portion (15g/½oz): 72 Kcal
3g fat (0.8g saturated)

Caster sugar 175g (6oz)
Golden syrup 75g (3oz)
Unsalted peanuts 175g (6oz)
Unsalted butter 15g (½oz)

Oil a baking sheet and fill a jug with boiling water.

Put the sugar and golden syrup into a heavy-based pan and add 125ml (4fl oz) cold water. Heat gently, stirring continuously, until the sugar has completely dissolved, occasionally brushing down the sides of the pan with hot water.

Add the peanuts to the sugar syrup and bring to the boil. Boil, without stirring, for 7–10 minutes until the mixture turns a rich golden caramel colour.

Immediately remove from the heat and add the butter. Do not stir, but mix into the caramel by tilting the pan. Quickly pour onto the oiled baking sheet. Leave to cool and set hard.

When cold, break into pieces and store in a jar or tin, interleaved with non-stick baking paper.

Cook's TIPS
Always keep a watchful eye when boiling sugar syrup. It can feel as though it is taking ages then it will suddenly begin to change colour around the edges then quickly darken all over.

Scan the
QR Code with a
smartphone for
an ingredients
shopping list

Makes 12 cakes

Time 35 minutes plus cooling

Per cake: 261 Kcal
17g fat (9.7g saturated)

Cappuccino Cakes

 (without cream)

Self-raising flour 175g (6oz)

Butter 110g (4oz), at room temperature

Caster sugar 110g (4oz)

Eggs 2, beaten

Milk 2 tbsp

Instant coffee 2 tsp, dissolved in 1 tsp boiling water

Cocoa powder 25g (1oz)

Salt a pinch

Double cream 150ml (¼ pint)

Icing sugar 1 tbsp

Milk chocolate curls made by running a swivel-bladed vegetable peeler along the underside of a chocolate bar

Preheat the oven to 180°C/160°fan/Gas 4. Line a patty tin with 12 paper cases.

In a large mixing bowl, mix the flour, butter, caster sugar, eggs, milk, coffee, cocoa and salt. Beat together until the mixture is smooth and has a dropping consistency.

Divide the mixture among the paper cases and bake for 15 minutes until well risen. Leave to cool on a wire rack.

Whisk together the cream and icing sugar until thick. Pipe or spoon the cream on top of the cooled cakes and sprinkle with chocolate curls.

Scan the
QR Code with a
smartphone for
an ingredients
shopping list

Cook's
TIPS

These cakes could also be topped with coffee flavoured buttercream instead of the cream.

These little coffee cakes from 2013 look so pretty they're perfect for serving on your best china when friends come to visit.

Moist and packed full of fruit, you can guarantee everyone will want a second square of this bread pud from the 2006 Diary.

Auntie Lou's Bread Pudding

Makes 16 squares

Time 1½ hours

Per square: 228 Kcal
9.8g fat (5.6g saturated)

Preheat the oven to 180°C/160°fan/Gas 4. Grease a 23cm (9in) square shallow ovenproof dish.

Soak the bread pieces in the milk in a large bowl for 10 minutes.

Add the rest of the ingredients and mix well. Transfer to the baking dish, spread evenly and bake for 45–50 minutes until the pudding is lightly browned and set in the centre.

Sprinkle with sugar and serve hot. Or leave to cool, cover and chill. Serve cold, cut into squares.

White bread, crust removed 225g (8oz), 2–3 days old, torn into small pieces

Milk 375ml (13fl oz)

Oranges 2, grated zest of both, juice of 1

Mixed spice 1 tbsp

Raisins 175g (6oz)

Sultanas 150g (5oz)

Chopped mixed peel 50g (2oz)

Ready-to-eat dried prunes 75g (3oz), chopped

Ready-to-eat dried apricots 75g (3oz), chopped

Glacé cherries 75g (3oz), quartered

Granulated sugar 25g (1oz) plus extra to sprinkle

Eggs 3, beaten

Butter 150g (5oz), melted

Black treacle 1–2 tbsp

Scan the **QR Code** with a smartphone for an ingredients shopping list

Bread pudding is one of those bakes meant to use up the leftovers, so if you don't have quite enough of one ingredient, mix and match with what you do have.

Christmas Flapjacks

Unsalted butter 175g (6oz)

Soft dark brown sugar
50g (2oz)

Golden syrup 90g (3½oz)

Rolled porridge oats
225g (8oz)

Pecan nuts 75g (3oz), chopped

Crystallised ginger 50g (2oz),
chopped

Maraschino or glacé cherries
75g (3oz), quartered

Preheat the oven to 200°C/180°fan/Gas 6. Grease a 22cm (8½in) round shallow cake tin and line the base with non-stick baking paper.

Put the butter, sugar and golden syrup into a large pan and stir over a moderate heat until the sugar has dissolved. Add all the remaining ingredients and mix well. Spoon into the prepared tin and spread evenly.

Bake for 25–30 minutes or until golden brown and firm to the touch. Leave to cool slightly, then run a palette knife around the edge to loosen. Cut into 12 triangles. Leave until completely cold, then cover and store in the fridge.

Scan the
QR Code with a
smartphone for
an ingredients
shopping list

Cook's
TIPS

Keep an eye on the flapjacks as they cook, and catch them just as they are a deep brown and just firm to the touch, they will firm up more as they cool. Flapjacks improve in flavour if kept for 1–2 days before eating.

With pecan nuts, ginger and cherries, these flapjacks from 2009 are really special. Pop in a tin, wrap in ribbon and give as a gift.

A delicious twist on the ubiquitous mince pie, these little morsels topped with marzipan from 2014 are perfect for the festive season.

Mince Pies with Marzipan

Makes 24
Time 35 minutes
Per pie: 196 Kcal
10g fat (4.7g saturated)

Preheat the oven to 180°C/160°fan/Gas 4.

Tip all the ingredients except the marzipan and mincemeat into a food processor and blend to make a smooth dough. Divide the dough in half and roll out each batch on a lightly floured surface. Using an 8cm (3in) fluted cutter, stamp out 24 rounds and use to line mince pie tins. Chill in the fridge while rolling out the topping.

Roll out the marzipan on a lightly floured surface and cut out 24 small stars measuring about 5cm (2in) across the furthest points.

Pop a spoonful of mincemeat into each pastry case, top with a marzipan star and bake for 12–15 minutes until golden and cooked.

Serve warm, dusted with a little sifted icing sugar.

Plain flour 225g (8oz)
Ground almonds 50g (2oz)
Icing sugar 75g (3oz), plus extra to dust
Butter 175g (6oz), diced
Egg yolk 1 medium
Marzipan 150g (5oz)
Mincemeat 450g (1lb)

Cook's TIPS Short of time, or don't like making pastry? Then cheat and use 500g (1lb 2oz) of ready-made sweet pastry.

Scan the **QR Code** with a smartphone for an ingredients shopping list

Makes 24 squares

Time 1½ hours plus cooling

Per square: 321 Kcal
20g fat (8.4g saturated)

Sweet shortcrust (dessert)
pastry 500g packet

Mincemeat 350-400g (12-14oz)

Butter 250g (9oz), softened

Caster sugar 250g (9oz)

Eggs 5 medium, beaten

Self-raising flour 125g (4½oz)

Ground almonds 125g (4½oz)

Almond extract 1 tsp

Icing sugar to dust

Mincemeat Bakewell Squares

Preheat the oven to 180°C/160°fan/Gas 4. Line the base and sides of a 26 x 38 x 2.5cm (10 x 15 x 1in) baking tray with non-sticking baking paper, leaving the paper about 5cm (2in) above the top of the tin.

Roll out the pastry on a lightly floured surface to a rectangle a little larger than the baking tray, then lift into the tray and push the pastry into the sides, corners and edges. Bake for 8–10 minutes until a very light golden colour.

Spoon the mincemeat onto the pastry while it's still warm and spread thinly until it just covers the pastry.

Using an electric mixer, beat together the butter and caster sugar until pale and creamy. Beat in the eggs a little at a time, adding a tablespoon of flour to prevent the mixture from curdling. Fold in the almonds, flour and almond extract. Spoon over the mincemeat and spread evenly.

Bake for 30–40 minutes until golden and firm to the touch. Leave to cool. Remove from the tray and peel away the paper, then cut into 24 squares. Dust lightly with icing sugar just before serving.

Scan the
QR Code with a
smartphone for
an ingredients
shopping list

You could use a layer of fruity jam instead of the mincemeat if you prefer.

A delicious recipe that proves mincemeat is not just for Christmas. This 2015 bake has a crisp pastry base, succulent mincemeat and a fluffy sponge topping.

From 1992, this moist banana & pecan cake,
packed with fruit, is a delicious teatime treat.

Banana & Pecan Cake

Makes 16 squares
Time 1¼ hours
Per square: 255 Kcal
11g fat (4.3g saturated)

Butter 110g (4oz)

Caster sugar 225g (8oz)

Eggs 3, separated

Peeled ripe bananas 225g (8oz), mashed

Buttermilk 150ml (¼ pint)

Plain flour 225g (8oz)

Baking powder 2 tsp

Sultanas 175g (6oz)

Pecan nut halves 90g (3½oz)

Preheat the oven to 180°C/160°fan/Gas 4. Grease a 20cm (8in) square cake tin and line with non-stick baking paper.

Cream the butter and sugar together until light and fluffy. Beat in the egg yolks, bananas and buttermilk. Add the flour, baking powder and sultanas and beat until smooth.

Whisk the egg whites until stiff and fold into the cake batter. Pour into the prepared tin and arrange the nuts on top. Bake for 1 hour or until a skewer comes out clean.

Leave to cool in the tin for 10 minutes before turning out. Cut into squares to serve.

Cook's TIPS

Ovens do vary, so check on the cake after 40 minutes and turn so that the cake browns evenly, if needed. If your oven is very hot, cover the top of the cake loosely with foil if you think it may brown too quickly.

Scan the **QR Code** with a smartphone for an ingredients shopping list

Makes 16 squares

Time 1¼ hours plus cooling

Per square: 246 Kcal
10g fat (6.2g saturated)

Butter 175g (6oz), softened

Golden caster sugar 175g (6oz)

Lemon 1, grated zest and juice

Eggs 3

Self-raising flour 225g (8oz)

Baking powder 1 tsp

Fondant icing sugar 225g (8oz)

Jelly oranges and lemons, sliced, to decorate

Summer Fête Lemon Cake

Preheat the oven to 180°C/160°fan/Gas 4. Grease an 18cm (7in) square cake tin and line with non-stick baking paper.

Using an electric mixer, beat together the butter, caster sugar, lemon zest, 1 tablespoon of lemon juice, eggs, flour and baking powder. Spoon into the prepared tin and bake for 35–45 minutes until firm to the touch.

Leave to cool in the tin for 10 minutes before turning out onto a wire rack to cool completely.

Sift the icing sugar into a bowl and gradually beat in enough lemon juice (and water, if necessary) to make a smooth thick icing. Spoon on top of the cake and spread evenly with a knife. Decorate with jelly slices and leave to set. Cut into squares.

Scan the **QR Code** with a smartphone for an ingredients shopping list

Cook's
TIPS

For a St Clements cake, add the grated zest of ½ lemon and ½ an orange, plus the juice of 1 lemon.

A light lemony sponge with fondant icing from the 2014 Dairy Diary, perfect for a cake or bake sale or for serving friends.

This light and fluffy, zesty citrus sponge from the 1998 Diary is topped with fondant icing and sugar flowers, and filled with a decadent and delicious orange clotted cream.

Orange Cake

Serves 12
Time 50 minutes plus cooling
Per slice: 434 Kcal
23g fat (14g saturated)

Preheat the oven to 180°C/160°fan/Gas 4 and grease two 20cm (8in) diameter sandwich tins.

Cream the butter and sugar together until pale and fluffy and then gradually beat in the eggs. Sift the flour and baking powder into the mixture and fold in with the orange zest and half the juice.

Divide the cake mixture between the prepared tins and bake for 25-30 minutes until firm to touch. Cool on a wire rack.

Spread one cake with marmalade and then spoon over the cream. Top with the other cake.

Make the icing by beating the remaining orange juice, a little at a time, into the icing sugar to give a thick spreadable icing. Spread over the cake and decorate with sugar flowers.

Butter 225g (8oz), softened

Caster sugar 175g (6oz)

Eggs 3, beaten

Self-raising flour 275g (10oz)

Baking powder 1 tsp

Oranges 1½ large, finely grated zest and juice

Marmalade 3 tbsp

Clotted cream 110g (4oz)

Icing sugar 200g (7oz)

Sugar flowers to decorate

Cook's TIPS

This cake has been sandwiched with clotted cream but 150ml (¼ pint) double cream could also be used. Whip until the cream forms soft swirls then spoon over the marmalade spread cake and top with the second cake or serve with just the marmalade filling if preferred.

Scan the **QR Code** with a smartphone for an ingredients shopping list

Serves 12

Time 2½ hours plus cooling

Per slice: 423 Kcal
14g fat (5.6g saturated)

Boiled Fruit Cake

Mixed dried fruit 350g (12oz)

Glacé cherries 150g (5oz), chopped

Chopped mixed peel 50g (2oz)

Walnuts 50g (2oz), chopped

Soft brown sugar 175g (6oz)

Butter 110g (4oz)

Mixed spice 1 tsp

Bicarbonate of soda ½ tsp

Milk 300ml (½ pint)

Self-raising flour 350g (12oz), sifted

Eggs 2, beaten

Walnut halves 10

Glacé cherries 5, halved

Preheat the oven to 160°C/140°fan/Gas 3. Grease a 20cm (8in) round deep-sided cake tin, line with non-stick baking paper and grease again.

Put the dried fruit, cherries, peel, walnuts, sugar, butter, spice, bicarbonate of soda and milk into a saucepan. Bring to the boil and simmer for 5 minutes. Cool to blood heat.

Stir in the flour and eggs. Turn the cake mixture into the prepared tin and decorate with walnut and cherry halves. Wrap the outside of the tin with baking paper.

Bake for 40 minutes, then reduce the oven temperature to 150°C/130°fan/Gas 2 and bake for a further 1½ hours or until a skewer comes out clean. Cover with foil halfway through cooking if the top is browning too much.

Leave to cool in the tin for 5 minutes, then turn out onto a wire rack, remove the paper and leave until completely cold before storing or serving.

Scan the **QR Code** with a smartphone for an ingredients shopping list

Cook's TIPS

A fruit cake is one of the few cakes that just gets better and better stored in a tin. For a Dundee-style cake topping decorate with rings of blanched almonds.

This rich, moist fruit cake from 1983 is a perennial Dairy Diary favourite.

A layered bake with walnuts and cinnamon, this streusel cake is taken from the 1984 Diary.

Streusel Cake

Serves 12

Time 1 hour

Per square: 258 Kcal
11g fat (5.3g saturated)

Butter 110g (4oz)
Caster sugar 175g (6oz)
Egg 1
Milk 150ml (¼ pint)
Self-raising flour 225g (8oz)
Soft brown sugar 75g (3oz)
Ground cinnamon 1 tsp
Walnuts 50g (2oz), chopped

Preheat the oven to 180°C/160°fan/Gas 4. Grease a 28 x 18cm (11 x 7in) cake tin and line with non-stick baking paper.

Cream 75g (3oz) of the butter with the caster sugar until light and fluffy. Beat in the egg and milk and carefully fold in 200g (7oz) of the flour. Put half the mixture into the prepared tin.

Make the topping by rubbing together the remaining butter with the remaining flour, the brown sugar and cinnamon. Add the walnuts. Sprinkle half the topping over the mixture in the tin. Cover with the remaining cake mixture then sprinkle with the remaining topping.

Bake for 35–40 minutes until a skewer inserted into the centre of the cake comes out clean. Cool slightly in the tin then remove to a wire rack to cool completely. Remove the baking paper and cut into 12 squares.

Used soft light muscovado sugar for this or if you don't have any then use demerara instead.

Scan the **QR Code** with a smartphone for an ingredients shopping list

Serves 8

Time 2 hours

Per slice: 466 Kcal
20g fat (12g saturated)

Spiced Apple Cake

Butter 175g (6oz), at room temperature

Soft light brown sugar 175g (6oz)

Self-raising flour 250g (9oz)

Mixed spice 2 tsp

Eggs 3, lightly beaten

Sultanas 150g (5oz)

Cooking apples 2, peeled, cored and thinly sliced

Lemon juice 2 tsp

Demerara sugar 25g (1oz)

Runny honey 1 tbsp

Preheat the oven to 180°C/160°fan/Gas 4. Grease and line the base of a 23cm (9in) springform tin with a circle of non-stick baking paper.

Add the butter and sugar to a bowl or base of a food mixer and cream together until light and fluffy.

Mix the flour and spice together in a second bowl. Gradually beat in alternate spoonfuls of beaten egg and flour to the butter and sugar until both have all been added and the cake mix is smooth.

Stir in the sultanas then spoon the cake mixture into the prepared tin and spread the top level. Arrange the apple slices, overlapping in rings over the top. Drizzle with a little lemon juice to stop them going brown then sprinkle with the demerara sugar.

Bake for about 1¼ hours or until well risen and a skewer comes out cleanly when inserted into the centre of the cake.

Leave to cool in the tin for 10 minutes then loosen the edge, remove the tin and lining paper and transfer to a wire rack. Drizzle the honey over the top and leave to cool.

Scan the **QR Code** with a smartphone for an ingredients shopping list

Cook's TIPS

Check on the cake halfway through cooking and cover the top with foil if the apples look as though they are browning a little too quickly.

*From the 1985 Dairy Diary, this beautiful
spiced fruit cake with a layer of sliced apple
is perfect with a spoonful of cream.*

The classic checkerboard cake flavoured with coffee and topped with marzipan and crystallised ginger, from the 2011 Dairy Diary, is surprisingly simple to make.

Coffee Battenberg

Serves 6–8
Time 1 hour plus cooling
Per slice: 633 Kcal
28g fat (12g saturated)

Preheat the oven to 180°C/160°fan/Gas 4. Grease a 20cm (8in) square cake tin. Line the tin with foil, making a pleat in the centre to the height of the tin (supported with cardboard) to divide in half; grease the foil.

Beat the butter and sugar together until light and fluffy. Gradually beat in the eggs and flour alternately until smooth. Transfer half the mixture to another bowl. Fold coffee essence into one half and milk into the other half.

Spoon the coffee-flavoured mixture into one side of the tin and the plain mixture into the other side. Bake for 30–35 minutes until risen and firm to the touch, then turn onto a wire rack to cool.

Trim the cakes to the same size and cut both in half lengthways. Spread the side of one brown piece of cake with marmalade and gently push together with a plain piece. Brush more marmalade on top of both and place the remaining brown piece on the plain piece and vice versa.

Dust a sheet of non-stick baking paper with sifted icing sugar and roll out the marzipan until large enough to wrap around the cake. Spread the marzipan with marmalade and carefully roll around the cake, smoothing in place. Trim off excess marzipan then crimp along the edges. Decorate with crystallised ginger, if using.

Butter 175g (6oz)
Caster sugar 175g (6oz)
Eggs 3, beaten
Self-raising flour 175g (6oz)
Coffee essence 4 tsp
Milk 1 tbsp
Ginger marmalade 10 tbsp
Icing sugar to dust
Marzipan 450g (1lb)
Crystallised ginger 2 pieces, roughly chopped, to decorate (optional)

Cook's **TIPS** For a traditional coloured Battenburg cake, colour half the cake mixture with a little pink food colouring then sandwich the strips of cake together with a little sieved strawberry jam before wrapping in marzipan.

Scan the **QR Code** with a smartphone for an ingredients shopping list

Serves 12
Time 3 hours plus cooling
Per slice: 457 Kcal
16g fat (8.3g saturated)

Simnel Cake

Butter 175g (6oz)
Caster sugar 175g (6oz)
Eggs 3, beaten
Plain flour 250g (9oz), sifted
Mixed spice 1 tsp
Mixed dried fruit 450g (1lb)
Milk 2 tbsp
Marzipan 250g (9oz), rolled
Apricot jam 3 tbsp
Sugar-coated chocolate eggs
to decorate (optional)

Preheat the oven to 160°C/140°fan/Gas 3. Grease an 18cm (7in) round cake tin and line with non-stick baking paper.

Cream the butter and sugar together until light and fluffy. Gradually beat in the eggs. Sift in the flour and spice and mix to a smooth soft consistency. Add the dried fruit and milk and mix well.

Spoon the mixture into the prepared tin and bake for 1 hour, then reduce the oven temperature to 150°C/130°fan/Gas 2 and bake for a further 1½ hours or until the cake is firm to the touch.

Leave to cool in the tin for 10 minutes, then turn out onto a wire rack to cool completely.

Roll the marzipan out to an 18cm (7in) diameter circle, 1cm (½in) thick, and make 11 marzipan balls with the remainer. Brush the top of the cake with apricot jam and lay the marzipan circle on top. Pinch the edges to give a fluted effect.

Decorate with the marzipan balls and sugar-coated chocolate eggs, if you like.

Scan the
QR Code with a
smartphone for
an ingredients
shopping list

Cook's
TIPS

For a citrus burst you could also stir in the grated zest of ½ lemon and ½ small orange when adding the dried fruit to the cake mixture.

*Simnel cake dates back to medieval times.
This version is a little more recent – from 2000
and is traditionally eaten at Easter.*

Minty Lemon Sorbet Tea

Serves 4   Time 5 minutes plus cooling

Per glass: 59 Kcal,   0.2g fat (0g saturated)

Darjeeling tea 600ml (1 pint), hot and strong
Sprigs of mint 3
Golden granulated sugar to taste
Lemon sorbet 4 scoops
Lemon 1, sliced
Strawberries and mint sprigs to decorate

Pour the hot tea into a jug, add the mint sprigs and stir in the sugar to taste. Leave to brew and cool completely.

When ready to serve, remove the mint sprigs. Scoop the lemon sorbet into four tall glasses and pour in the tea. Decorate with strawberries and mint and serve immediately.

Fruity Gin

Serves 24   Time 45 minutes plus 4–5 months infusing and storing
Per 25ml shot: 79 Kcal, 0g fat (0g saturated)

Blueberries 450g (1lb)
or Kumquats 450g (1lb), sliced and pips removed
or Plums 500g (1lb 2oz), stoned and sliced
Gin 600ml (1 pint)
Light muscovado sugar 150g (5oz)

Put your chosen fruit into a large jar with a tight-fitting lid.

Pour the gin into the jar, add the sugar, stir well until the sugar has dissolved and then cover with the lid and store in a cool, dark, airy cupboard for 3–4 months. Stir once a week until the sugar has completely dissolved.

When the gin has developed a good, fruity flavour, strain it through muslin into a large jug or bowl. Discard the fruit and then pour the gin into sterilised bottles for storing.

Store the gin for at least 1 month before drinking. It will keep for several years.

Serve well chilled, poured over ice cubes.

Cook's tips Instead of the fruits suggested, use sloes to make sloe gin. You will need 500g (1lb 2oz). Sloes are in season in autumn.

Tropical Fruit Shake

Serves 2   Time 5 minutes

Per glass: 222 Kcal, 7.5g fat (4.7g saturated)

Banana 1
Orange juice 2 tbsp
Pineapple juice 2 tbsp
Milk 300ml (½ pint), chilled
Vanilla ice cream 2 scoops
Grated orange zest (optional)

Mash the banana with the orange and pineapple juices. Blend together with the milk.

Put a scoop of ice cream into each glass, pour in the fruity milk and add the orange zest, if using. Serve immediately.

Piña Colada

Serves 1   Time 5 minutes

Per glass: 225 Kcal, 16g fat (10g saturated)

White rum 1 tbsp
Coconut liqueur 1 tbsp
Pineapple juice 1 tbsp
Double cream 1 tbsp
Crushed ice

Put all the ingredients into a blender and blend until thick and frothy. Serve immediately.

Peach Cream Liqueur

Serves 4   Time 5 minutes plus chilling

Per glass: 263 Kcal, 14g fat (9.1g saturated)

Single cream 300ml (½ pint)
Peach schnapps 150ml (¼ pint)
Vanilla extract ½ tsp
Caster sugar 1 tbsp

Mix all the ingredients together, stirring until the sugar has dissolved. Chill well.

Serve in small liqueur glasses.

This will keep in the fridge for 3–4 days.

Cook's tips Instead of peach schnapps, try other fruit liqueurs, such as raspberry or blackcurrant. If you use a very sweet liqueur such as apricot brandy, omit the sugar.

Perfect Peach

Serves 2   Time 5 minutes

Per cup: 263 Kcal, 5g fat (3.2g saturated)

Milk 600ml (1 pint)
Peaches in natural juice 410g can, drained
Light soft brown sugar 2 tbsp
Almond essence a few drops

Put all the ingredients into a blender or food processor and blend until smooth.

Pour into a pan, heat thoroughly and serve.

Hazelnut Hot Chocolate

Serves 2   Time 5 minutes

Per cup: 267 Kcal, 13g fat (5g saturated)

Milk 600ml (1 pint)
Chocolate hazelnut spread 3 tbsp
Orange ¼, finely grated zest

Heat the milk in a pan with the chocolate spread, stirring until dissolved. Stir in the orange zest, pour into cups and serve immediately.

Hot Pear Milk

Serves 1   Time 5 minutes

Per cup: 174 Kcal, 3.4g fat (2.1g saturated)

Canned pear halves, drained
Milk 200ml (7fl oz)
Ground cinnamon a pinch

Put all the ingredients into a blender or food processor and blend until smooth.

Pour into a pan, heat thoroughly but do not boil. Serve immediately, sprinkled with a little extra cinnamon.

Spiced Hot Chocolate

Serves 2   Time 5 minutes

Per cup: 347 Kcal, 20g fat (12g saturated)

Milk 600ml (1 pint)
Drinking chocolate 3 tbsp, plus extra to serve
Ground cinnamon ½ tsp
Mixed spice a large pinch
Double cream, whipped

Put the milk in a pan and bring to the boil. Whisk in the drinking chocolate and spices.

Pour into cups and serve topped with whipped cream and a little sifted drinking chocolate.

After Eight Milk

Serves 2   Time 5 minutes

Per cup: 152 Kcal, 4.3g fat (2.7g saturated)

Hot milk 400ml (14fl oz)
Drinking chocolate 4 tsp, plus extra to serve (optional)
Peppermint essence a few drops
Grated chocolate to serve (optional)

Put the milk in a pan and bring to the boil. Whisk in the drinking chocolate and peppermint essence.

Pour into cups and serve topped with grated chocolate, if you like.

A

After Eight milk 171

almonds, mincemeat Bakewell squares 152

apples

broccoli & apple soup 8

butterscotch apple pie 96

liver special 46

rustic raspberry crumble 94

sausagemeat Yorkshire 74

spiced apple cake 164

stuffed pork fillet 114

apricots

Auntie Lou's bread pudding 146

Calypso puddings 98

frozen Christmas pudding 82

hot Swiss trifle 92

turkey en croûte 66

asparagus

chicken & asparagus pie 64

sea bass with asparagus 36

aubergine, vegetarian moussaka 52

B

bacon

bacon wraps 100

eggy bread BLT 9

roast chicken with cheese & peanut stuffing 60

savoury muffins 138

banana

banana & pecan cake 154

banana cream pie 88

beans

chilli beans with wedges 32

chilli beef tacos 48

cottage pie with baked beans 18

gourmet beans on toast 38

beef

boeuf Stroganoff 80

chilli beef tacos 48

cottage pie with baked beans 18

steak en croûte 118

biscuits, dainty iced gingerbread 140

boeuf Stroganoff 80

bread

Auntie Lou's bread pudding 146

eggy bread BLT 9

gourmet beans on toast 38

Irish soda bread 136

naan bread 116

pigs in blankets 16

broccoli

broccoli & apple soup 8

chicken & broccoli lasagne 62

butterscotch apple pie 96

C

cabbage, treacle-glazed red cabbage 68

cakes

banana & pecan cake 154

boiled fruit cake 160

cappuccino cakes 144

coffee Battenberg 166

orange cake 158

simnel cake 168

spiced apple cake 164

streusel cake 162

summer fête lemon cake 156

calypso puddings 98

candy rice pudding 22

cappuccino cakes 144

cauliflower & potato curry 26

cheese

cheese & tomato tasty 8

chicken & broccoli lasagne 62

chilli beans with wedges 32

family fish pie 54

gourmet beans on toast 38

ham & cheese soufflé 108

mushroom ramekins 102

pasta supper 14

pepperami muffins 9

perfect potatoes 30

pork crumble 70

roast chicken with cheese & peanut stuffing 60

sausage & leek supper 72

sausagemeat Yorkshire 74

savoury croissants 9

stuffed pork fillet 114

toastie yogurt surprise 9

two cheese fondue 120

vegetarian moussaka 52

cheesecake, white chocolate 126

chicken

chicken & asparagus pie 64

chicken & broccoli lasagne 62

chicken & corn soup 8

chicken Kievs 12

lemon chicken 42

pesto chicken 112

roast chicken with cheese & peanut stuffing 60

chicken liver pâté 106

chilli beans with wedges 32

chilli beef tacos 48

chocolate

chocolate fondue 120

chocolate maple yule log 84

chocolate pear flan 86

frozen Christmas pudding 82

hazelnut hot chocolate 171

iced mocha soufflé 122

spiced hot chocolate 171

white chocolate cheesecake 126

Christmas flapjack 148

Christmas pudding, frozen 82

chutney
  curried supper eggs 34
  toastie yogurt surprise 9
cinnamon pancakes 24
coconut, chocolate pear flan 86
coffee
  cappuccino cakes 144
  coffee Battenberg 166
  iced mocha soufflé 122
cottage pie with baked beans 18
courgettes, vegetarian moussaka 52
crumble
  pork 70
  rustic raspberry 94
cucumber
  baked salmon 56
  smoked salmon & dill filo tarts 104
curried supper eggs 34
curry
  cauliflower & potato curry 26
  kofta curry with naan bread 116
  lamb keema curry 44
custard
  hot Swiss trifle 92
  pear & ginger trifle 90
  queen of puddings 132
  raspberry amaretto trifle 124
  stripy jelly 20

D
dried fruit
  Auntie Lou's bread pudding 146
  boiled fruit cake 160
  Calypso puddings 98
  frozen Christmas pudding 82
  simnel cake 168
drinks 170–171

E
eggs
  banana cream pie 88
  cinnamon pancakes 24
  curried supper eggs 34
  eggy bread BLT 9
  ham & cheese soufflé 108
  Hollandaise sauce 110
  queen of puddings 132
  toastie yogurt surprise 9

F
fish
  baked salmon 56
  family fish pie 54
  gourmet beans on toast 38
  hollandaise salmon 110
  homemade fish fingers 10
  sea bass with asparagus 36
  smoked salmon & dill filo tarts 104
  spicy tuna plait 58
flapjack, Christmas 148
fondue
  chocolate 120
  two cheese 120
fruit
  Calypso puddings 98
  easy fruit brûlée 130
  fruity gin 170
  tropical fruit shake 170
fruit cake, boiled 160

G
gin, fruity 170
ginger cake, pear & ginger trifle 90
gingerbread, dainty iced 140
green beans, cauliflower & potato curry 26

H
ham
  ham & cheese soufflé 108
  lemon chicken 42
  pasta supper 14
  savoury croissants 9
  stuffed pork fillet 114
hazelnut hot chocolate 171
hollandaise salmon 110

I
ice cream, iced mocha soufflé 122
Irish soda bread 136

J
jelly, stripy 20

L
lamb
  kofta curry with naan bread 116
  lamb crown roast 76
  lamb keema curry 44
  minced lamb pie 78
lasagne, chicken & broccoli 62
leeks
  pork crumble 70
  sausage & leek supper 72
lemons
  double lemon puddings 134
  lemon chicken 42
  minty lemon sorbet tea 170
  summer fête lemon cake 156
lettuce, eggy bread BLT 9
liver
  chicken liver pâté 106
  liver special 46

m

marmalade, orange cake 158

marzipan
  coffee Battenberg 166
  mince pies with marzipan 150
  simnel cake 168

melon, bacon wraps 100

milk
  After Eight milk 171
  banana cream pie 88
  candy rice pudding 22
  cinnamon pancakes 24
  ham & cheese soufflé 108
  hazelnut hot chocolate 171
  hot pear milk 171
  spiced hot chocolate 171
  tropical fruit shake 170

mince pies with marzipan 150

mincemeat Bakewell squares 152

minty lemon sorbet tea 170

moussaka, vegetarian 52

muffins
  pepperami 9
  savoury 138

mushrooms
  beef Stroganoff 80
  chicken & asparagus pie 64
  mushroom ramekins 102
  pork crumble 70
  savoury croissants 9

n

noodles, peanut noodles 28

nuts
  banana & pecan cake 154
  boiled fruit cake 160
  chocolate maple yule log 84
  crunchy peanut brittle 142
  mincemeat Bakewell squares 152

peanut noodles 28

pesto chicken 112

roast chicken with cheese & peanut stuffing 60

spicy tuna plait 58

streusel cake 162

o

oats
  Christmas flapjack 148
  pork crumble 70

olives
  bacon wraps 100
  steak en croûte 118

onions, liver special 46

oranges
  frozen Christmas pudding 82
  orange cake 158

p

pancakes, cinnamon with blueberry sauce 24

pasta
  chicken & broccoli lasagne 62
  pasta supper 14

peach cream liqueur 170

peaches, perfect peach 171

peanuts
  crunchy peanut brittle 142
  peanut noodles 28
  roast chicken with cheese & peanut stuffing 60

pears
  chocolate pear flan 86
  hot pear milk 171
  pear & ginger trifle 90

peas, pasta supper 14

pecans
  banana & pecan cake 154
  chocolate maple yule log 84

pepperami muffins 9

peppers
  chilli beans with wedges 32
  liver special 46

pesto chicken 112

pies & tarts
  banana cream pie 88
  butterscotch apple pie 96
  chicken & asparagus 64
  chocolate pear flan 86
  cottage pie with baked beans 18
  family fish pie 54
  mince pies with marzipan 150
  minced lamb 78
  mincemeat Bakewell squares 152
  smoked salmon & dill filo tarts 104
  spicy tuna plait 58
  steak en croûte 118
  turkey en croûte 66

pigs in blankets 16

piña colada 170

pork
  pork crumble 70
  roast pork with fanned potatoes and treacle-glazed red cabbage 68
  stuffed pork fillet 114

potatoes
  cauliflower & potato curry 26
  chilli beans with wedges 32
  cottage pie with baked beans 18
  family fish pie 54
  lemon chicken 42
  perfect potatoes 30
  pesto chicken with roasted potatoes 112
  roast pork with fanned potatoes and treacle-glazed red cabbage 68
  sausage & leek supper 72
  sea bass with asparagus & roasted potatoes 36

prawns, eight minute prawns 40

prunes

   Auntie Lou's bread pudding 146

   bacon wraps 100

   calypso puddings 98

   frozen Christmas pudding 82

puddings *see also* pies & tarts; trifle

   calypso puddings 98

   chocolate fondue 120

   double lemon puddings 134

   easy fruit brûlée 130

   queen of puddings 132

   raspberry amaretto trifle 124

   white chocolate cheesecake 126

Q

queen of puddings 132

R

raspberries

   raspberry amaretto trifle 124

   rustic raspberry crumble 94

rice, candy rice pudding 22

roast chicken with cheese & peanut stuffing 60

S

salmon

   baked salmon 56

   hollandaise salmon 110

   smoked salmon & dill filo tarts 104

sandwiches, eggy bread BLT 9

sauces

   blueberry 24

   hollandaise 110

   pesto 112

sausagemeat Yorkshire 74

sausages

   pigs in blankets 16

   sausage & leek supper 72

   turkey en croûte 66

savoury croissants 9

sea bass with asparagus 36

simnel cake 168

smoked salmon & dill filo tarts 104

snacks

   eggy bread BLT 9

   pepperami muffins 9

   savoury croissants 9

   toastie yogurt surprise 9

soufflé, ham & cheese 108

soups

   broccoli & apple soup 8

   chicken & corn soup 8

   Spanish tomato soup 8

Spanish tomato soup 8

steak en croûte 118

strawberry puffs 128

streusel cake 162

stripy jelly 20

swede, family fish pie 54

sweetcorn

   cauliflower & potato curry 26

   chicken & broccoli lasagne 62

   chicken & corn soup 8

   liver special 46

   perfect potatoes 30

Swiss trifle 92

T

tea, minty lemon sorbet 170

toastie yogurt surprise 9

tomatoes

   cheese & tomato tasty 8

   chilli beans with wedges 32

   chilli beef tacos 48

   eggy bread BLT 9

   lamb keema curry 44

savoury muffins 138

   Spanish tomato soup 8

   vegetarian moussaka 52

trifle

   hot Swiss 92

   pear & ginger 90

   raspberry amaretto 124

tropical fruit shake 170

tuna

   gourmet beans on toast 38

   spicy tuna plait 58

turkey en croûte 66

V

vegetarian moussaka 52

W

walnuts

   boiled fruit cake 160

   pesto chicken 112

   spicy tuna plait 58

   streusel cake 162

white chocolate cheesecake 126

Y

yogurt

   easy fruit brûlée 130

   toastie yogurt surprise 9

Yorkshire puddings with sausagemeat and apple 74

Thanks to

Executive	Editor Nick Rowe
Managing Editor	Emily Davenport
Editor	Maggie Ramsey
Photographers	Steve Lee
	Frank Weider
Food Stylist	Sara Lewis
Props Stylist	Olivia Wardle
Designer	Graham Meigh

Recipes taken from Dairy Diaries

Proof Reader	Aune Butt
Indexer	Ruth Ellis
Nutritional Consultant	Paul McArdle
Recipe Testers	Richard Davenport
	Katy Hackforth
	Claire Nadin
	Laura Pickering
Production	Cath Linter

Eaglemoss Ltd
Electra House, Electra Way, Crewe, Cheshire, CW1 6GL
Tel 01270 270050
www.dairydiary.co.uk
www.dairydiarychat.co.uk

First printed May 2016
© Eaglemoss Ltd
ISBN: 978-0-9932105-1-8
123456789